The Wife's Sister's Wee Boy

KEN THATCHER

©2023 Ken Thatcher
Layout/design by Neil Roddy - www.fudgedesigns.co.uk
Cover design by Bridget Murray
Printed by Bizzprint

The moral rights of the authors and contributors have been asserted in accordance with
the Copyright, Designs and Patents Act, 1998.
First published November 2023.
Colmcille Press, Ráth Mór Centre, Derry BT48 0LZ
Managing Editor Garbhán Downey
www.colmcillepress.com

Colmcille Press gratefully acknowledges the support of Creggan Enterprises Limited
and the John Bryson Foundation.

The John Bryson
Foundation

RÁTH MÓR
Creggan Enterprises

ISBN 978-1-914009-40-2
A CIP copy for this book is available from the British Library.

ACKNOWLEDGEMENTS

The motivation for this memoir came from the late Sean McMahon who insisted that I could and should do it and for that confidence I thank him. I'm just sorry it took a while to get around to it. The most important reason for tackling such a task stems from a desire to let my children and grandchildren know how their father and grandfather became the person that he is. I have taken great pleasure in this trip down memory lane and have smiled often as I reflected on past events. I would thank all those whom I have remembered and apologise if I have mis-remembered some of the details.

My time as a pupil at Foyle College was a happy one. To all of those who did their best with me I owe you thanks although at the time I might not have expressed it. A debt of gratitude is owed to Foyle Books for assisting with the publication of the book. To those who offered encouragement and advice, I trust I have accepted it willingly.

Finally, thanks to Margaret, Emma, Catherine, Lee, Martin, Harry, Jack and Patrick, just for being there.

FOREWORD
By Art Byrne

How important background influences are in the making of us!
Ken Thatcher's blow-in sailor father gave him family to visit in England.
But his mother's background in the Derry side of the River Foyle was
so much more influential. Deciding that a little boy could cross the
Craigavon Bridge to attend Model Primary School.

That the family should soon move from the Waterside to a house
on Nicholson Terrace. That they would attend his mother's Church
of Ireland church. Where he found a chair, boy scouts, a youth club,
and a rector who advised him to go to university. To study French, the
language a teacher in Foyle College had taught him to love. And his
mother's family connection made him work every summer on a farm in
Creevagh.

Of course, bit by bit he becomes aware of living in a divided town.
As a four year old he didn't know, when asked, was he a Protestant
or a Catholic! Later he understood there were different schools, hops,
snooker-halls, pubs. And discontent would explode in 1968 just two
days before he begins university at Magee College, Londonderry.

This is a wonderful memoir by a man who remained in his native
town, to be a teacher, broadcaster, and to set up a marvellous bookshop.

IN THE BEGINNING

As she wheeled the heavy pram bearing her infant son around the bend at Thompson's Corner, bracing herself for the final steep push which would bring her to the top of the hill at Altnagelvin, leaving only the easy descent past the recently constructed houses at Irish Street to her mother's home in Bond's Hill, she must have wondered just how it had all come about.

To know precisely how it had come to pass we need to go back about ten years and move to a distant land far from Drumahoe and the northwest of Ireland, to Palestine. Two shipmates who had been enjoying shore leave in the Holy Land were discussing plans for Christmas: one of them intended to go home, the other had no home as such to go to, having run away at the age of fourteen to join the Royal Navy. They both agreed that it would be a good idea to go to Derry, where the former lived with his father, mother, brothers, and sisters. And so, during Christmas week 1938, the man who was to be my father and his friend, later to be my uncle, arrived at the family home in Cedar Street. Goodness knows what his father and mother thought. Cedar Street was a row of rather modest two-up, two-down dwellings, one of which was the Bradley home which already housed five people.

Nevertheless, that is precisely how it all began. Apparently my father paid little attention to my mother nor she to him, but in later life when he and I were chatting one night he confessed that he believed he had met the girl with whom he was to spend the rest of his days. However, knowing that war was coming he had made a conscious decision to keep his powder dry and see if he survived the conflict. Later my mother would also confide in me that she had paid very little attention to her brother's English friend. There had after all been a certain age difference; she would have still been a teenager and he was about fifteen years older. They went their separate ways.

THE HIDDEN YEARS

The war was never much discussed in our house so most of what I have gleaned is from wider family members or friends. Very occasionally, little snippets of information would drop casually into a conversation.

For example, I know that there was an English soldier whom my mother had met at a church function who made an impression on her; it was mentioned once, casually, and never alluded to again. I gathered that my mother had been a serious young woman, never much minded to go dancing or participate in any great frivolity. At one point she had decided to travel to Scotland with the possibility of exploring the idea of becoming a nurse, this came to nothing but because wartime travel restrictions were imposed between the mainland and Northern Ireland, she found herself marooned in Scotland. She spent a considerable amount of time in Saltcoats where the family had connections. During this period of enforced exile she made lifelong friends with some local people whom we visited regularly in later life. After several months in Saltcoats she eventually managed to get home where she spent the remainder of the war working in a variety of offices.

My father's war I learned about from different sources – he seldom mentioned it. My uncle, he who had been in The Holy Land, once explained to me that some people had an easy war, others had a hard war. He had had an easy war: he spent most of it in a small naval craft patrolling the east coast of England, with a welcome break of several months in Reykjavik in a naval radio and reconnaissance station monitoring North Atlantic radio traffic. My father, on the other hand, had a hard war.

When the war began my father had risen to the rank of Chief Petty Officer of Signals. It was his job to communicate with other ships, or further afield, by using semaphore, lamps, running flags up the mast,

Morse Code, or radio, all of which meant that he was generally on the ship's bridge close to the captain or whoever was in command of the vessel. The bridge was always the prime target in any offensive action. In battle, this would have been the most dangerous part of the ship.

To sum up what I do know of his wartime experiences, I can say for a fact that ships on which he served were torpedoed and sunk or severely damaged on six occasions. Once his ship was sunk off the coast of Norway and he had to swim ashore in freezing seas. The survivors were hidden by the Norwegian resistance and rescued when English ships attacked the town of Narvik. The only thing he ever told me about that particular episode was that he had acquired a brilliant set of German binoculars from a captured German submariner but had had to let them go as he swam ashore as they were dragging his head under the waves. A small price to pay for salvation I thought but he talked about them often during my childhood. He was also one of those who sailed with the Russian convoys, protecting cargo ships bringing munitions and supplies to our Russian allies. When the weather in Derry became a bit chilly he would wax lyrical about the frozen seas of the Arctic Circle, when the entire ship might be covered in thick ice and waves crashing over the deck kept all hands indoors. He also served for some time in the Mediterranean and was present at the Battle of Tobruk, where he was mentioned in despatches. Indeed, he appears in a work about the battle entitled Tobruk Commando.

During his spell in the Mediterranean he was captured by the Italians and made a prisoner of war in Bari in southern Italy. This was one of the few episodes which I knew him to talk about willingly. He felt sorry for the Italian guards as they seemed just as miserable and hungry as he was. Due to this experience the notion of wasting food was anathema and ever afterwards in the Thatcher household every scrap of food which was edible had to be consumed. After some months he was repatriated as a result of a negotiated swap of prisoners.

The only wartime incident about which he spoke with any great gusto concerned shore leave at Gibraltar. All the time I knew my father he was a strict teetotaller but apparently this had not always been the case. It seems that during his shore leave in 'Gib' he had fallen in with some Russian sailors, one thing led to another and he had arrived back on his ship terribly drunk and on a stretcher. In the morning he was hauled up before the captain and given a dreadful dressing down, but as he turned to leave the captain told him he had single handedly improved British relationships with Russia no end due to whatever had taken place during the drinking spree.

Before the war he had served in the South China Sea, where on one occasion he had been to all intents and purposes left in charge of the entire field of operations. On hearing that a flotilla of pirates had been sighted close by, he sent the fleet to sea, forgetting that most of the hierarchy were participating in a gala evening on shore and therefore the fleet had set sail without the top brass. He never told me the consequences of his action but I always got the impression he had 'gotten away with it', as he often did. Much later in life, my mother and I were chatting and she recounted the following anecdote. In a dark moment my father had been reflecting on his wartime experiences and said rather tellingly that he had found it really hard to understand why comrades who were married with children were being mown down on either side of him, yet he survived with just a piece of shrapnel in his leg to remind him of those horrific days. Obviously he had witnessed events that stayed with him all his days, which he kept locked away and chose never to discuss.

MORE AND MORE CURIOUS

So the war came to an end and my father survived. Unlike many of his erstwhile shipmates my father was a career sailor and thus his life still lay with the navy. The next bit is a mystery. During the war my mother's family had moved from Cedar Street to Baronet Street. I found it fascinating that they should move from a quiet residential area to a street which had several enormous storage tanks filled with marine fuel on one side, right alongside the quay where countless frigates and destroyers were moored at a time when German air raids were a constant possibility.

For me, the greatest puzzle of all was how on earth did my father find her, he who had had no communication whatsoever with the family or anyone else throughout the war? A mystery it shall remain but find her he did and as a consequence my mother and he were married in Christ Church Infirmary Road on the 17th February 1947, with my uncle who had first brought my father to Derry before the war as his best man.

I have only one piece of information pertaining to the two years which elapsed before my arrival and that concerns the honeymoon. The happy couple had decided to go overseas to celebrate their wedding and so set off to Scotland and England, presumably to meet my father's relatives and my mother's friends in Scotland. The winter of 1947 had been a harsh one and the train bringing the happy couple back to the ferry at Stranraer was suddenly engulfed in snowdrifts, grinding to a halt in the hills just inland from the Scottish coast. Snowploughs tried to break through without success and as helicopters were probably in their infancy at this time, rescue by air was impossible. The story made the newspapers and was featured on the front page of some of the nationals. Both my father and mother were enthusiastic smokers so it was no surprise that photographs in the press revealed the following message written in the snow by my father: 'Send cigs and food'. It took two days for them to be rescued. Shortly afterwards they returned home to Derry and set up home in Mill Cottage, in the village of Drumahoe on the outskirts of the city.

MOVING ON

So it came to pass that my mother, after a rather difficult confinement which required her to take long spells of bed rest, was delivered of me on the third day of July 1949. By all accounts I was a pretty sturdy boy of around nine pounds weight and after a few days in the City and County Hospital I was brought home to Drumahoe.

Mill Cottage was bought as a project. My father was brought up in a small rural village in Somerset, the son of a farm labourer and sometime coal miner. At a young age his mother died and his father remarried; my father never got on with his stepmother and this eventually led to his running away from home. This rural upbringing gave him a lifelong connection with the land and I think that was what made Mill Cottage so attractive. At the time of purchase the house was habitable but in need of attention – what made it so desirable was that it was situated in a sizable plot of ground of which he saw the potential. The front garden bordered the main road out of town to Belfast and to the rear the land sloped down to the banks of the River Faughan. I think it must have stretched at least one hundred yards from the road to the riverbank and about twenty yards from one side to the other. The mill which gave the cottage its name sat to the left on the riverbank. Evidently my father had the vision to see what a rural idyll he might create, so in 1947 it became the family home.

Drumahoe in the early 1950s was nothing like the place it is today. First of all, the main road followed a different route from today's major thoroughfare. It wound its way from the city, whose limits ended at the newly built Irish Street Estate, over the hill and down past Glendermott Parish Church towards Thompson's Corner, across the bridge where the Three Mile House pub still stands, continuing out past Mill Cottage through Drumahoe village and past the Watery Brae, heading for Claudy and eventually Belfast. The village itself consisted of the local primary school, whose catchment area included most of the nearby farming families, Henderson's post office and a garage with a scattering of dwellings alongside a not-too-busy main thoroughfare. Nothing remotely like the densely populated area Drumahoe is today.

Obviously, I have no memory of my mother pushing me in the pram to visit her mother in Bond's Hill, but surprisingly I have many clear memories of our time in Drumahoe. The earliest of these revolve around life in our kitchen, not surprising as in those days it was usually the warmest room in the house. I recall crawling around the floor in my terry nappy playing in front of the range when all of a sudden I was screaming in pain. I had reversed up against the stove and eventually the heat had penetrated my nappy and left me with a rather scorched bottom. Luckily no permanent damage was done and a soothing lotion was applied, but I think some kind of screen was erected to avoid any repeat injury. My other very early memory also took place in the kitchen. My father was very fond of cats and our family pet Ginger used to sit beside me in my highchair, sharing my food when my mother wasn't looking. Not the kind of behaviour we would find in today's hypersensitive society but obviously it did me no harm.

Another vivid recollection finds me on my feet and toddling. My mother was entertaining visitors in the good room, I was left to my own devices and was pottering around the house. Suddenly I discovered a cake stand in the kitchen, groaning with delicacies destined for my mother's guests. The temptation was too much – I set to the cream buns, removing the cream with my fingers and cunningly replacing it with crusts which had been sliced off the fancy sandwiches prepared for the guests. I was horrified when my deception failed and I was dispatched to my bedroom to reflect on my misdemeanours.

Our time at Mill Cottage is forever imbued with magical memories and none more so than the first Christmas which I can recall. It was a chilly, frosty night and I was sitting in our kitchen with my mother and Ginger. Suddenly there was a wild banging and hammering at the front door. Since my father had gone to town on an errand there were just the two of us in the house. I clung to my mother's skirt as we went to the front door. As she cautiously opened it, there, standing against the wall was a Christmas tree. Where had it come from? Who had been banging on the door? My mother stepped outside but there was no one to be seen, not a sound to be heard. We edged nervously round the house towards the kitchen door. As we rounded the corner we were once again astonished. There, strung between the two poles of the washing line, was a string of fairy lights twinkling in the frosty air. We made our way back into the kitchen still breathless from these inexplicable events. By then my father had returned from his errand in town and I couldn't wait to recount our adventure. That was the first and possibly the best of my Christmas memories.

Life in Drumahoe in my mind remains mostly a succession of agreeable experiences. I'm sure that bad things happened but most have evidently been erased as time rolled by. One event does stick in my mind. Between us and the next house along was a small stretch of uncultivated land where I would sometimes play with my friend who lived next door. One day as we played his father came out to saw some logs and inadvertently, as I looked on and my friend held the wood steady, he sawed off the tip of his finger. I ran back to the house screaming in horror. After being comforted by my mother it was made clear that this had been a practical joke. It transpired that my friend's father had bought a pretend severed finger in a joke shop and decided to play a trick at my expense. I saw less of my little friend after that.

There is one other rather unpleasant experience from that time which lives with me to this day. Apparently I was rather prone to sore throats and as a consequence the doctor decided that the most effective remedy would be the removal of my tonsils. Altnagelvin Hospital had not yet progressed beyond the architect's drawing board, so we were served by either The City and County Hospital on Infirmary Road or the lesser-known Roe Valley Hospital in Limavady. The Roe Valley was to be my destination. Travel was not quite as easy as it is today and getting to Limavady necessitated the borrowing of a car. I was in a ward with a number of other children and was rather apprehensive when my turn came to be left on my own in the company of strangers for the first time in my life.

I recall little of my stay in hospital but what does remain is indelible. I recollect lying on a trolley being wheeled to the operating table and being encouraged to fall asleep. I then remember blinking beneath a powerful light and finding a man wearing a mask holding my mouth open with some kind of utensil which he had inserted in my throat. He looked a bit astonished, as did his colleagues, but he whispered to me to go back to sleep, which I did. Next time I woke up I was back on my hospital bed lying with my head on a blood-soaked pillow. I did a lot of crying despite the nurses' kind words and efforts to console me. I don't think it was the pain which drew the tears, it was the feeling of loneliness, which wouldn't recede until a few days later when I was back in the comfort of my own house in Drumahoe.

Throughout the time we lived at Mill Cottage my father was still on active duty with the Royal Navy. I have no idea where or how this happened but I do recall that for short periods of time he would be away from home. When he was at home he was extremely active around the house and garden. His rural childhood seemed never to have left him and as a consequence he appeared to derive great pleasure from his garden. He planted apple and plum trees and set the enormous lawn which stretched from the front of the house to the main road. He had cleared the ground, dug it over and raked it out by himself – no mean feat. Most of it now lies under the realigned A6. He also kept some poultry, more of which later.

To the rear of the house ran the River Faughan, where I was allowed to sit and fish along the bank. It's hard to imagine that no one blinked an eye at the thought of a three-year-old, unattended, clutching a rod and line along the bank of a fast-flowing river. (I suspect I may have been the subject of some discreet surveillance.) The Faughan is a particularly important salmon and trout river and I recall being greeted cheerfully by the many anglers who would pass me by. It was only in later life I realised that one of the prerequisites for successful angling was to at least have a hook on the end of one's line.

One thing about my father which remains an enigma was his love of antiques. You would think that someone who had no permanent home would have found it difficult to house a collection of antique furniture and objets d'art but collect them he did. My earliest encounter with the world of antiques happened in our hallway at Mill Cottage. I had been left to amuse myself and was playing with a brush which my mother had been using earlier in the morning. Halfway along the hall stood a grandfather clock; a toy with which I had been playing had been inadvertently swept under the clock and I used the brush to try and poke it out again. This was my first lesson in physics and levers. Before I knew it I had upended the clock and was only saved from serious injury by the width of the hall, which prevented the clock from pinning me to the floor or worse. My father took the disaster with his usual equanimity; the clock never chimed again.

At some stage my mother must have thought it was time to return to work and so a plan was hatched for my grandmother to look after me at Mill Cottage. No doubt the plan worked well for a while but one day disaster struck. By this time my father had installed a henhouse. I remember it as quite a sizeable affair, big enough for an adult to stand in with little out-shots to the side where hens could lay and the eggs be collected without any need to enter the shed. For some reason my granny had gone to collect some eggs but rather than do it from outside she went inside with the hens. To my horror the wind caught the door and blew it closed, causing the wooden catch to drop and lock shut.

It took a few moments for the extent of the disaster to become apparent but very soon Granny realised what had happened and that her predicament was rather serious. I was too small to reach the latch to open the door and Granny was too big and probably too old to attempt to squirm her way through the out-shots at the side of the shed. The situation was only resolved when my mother returned some hours later. Inexplicably, I was somehow implicated in the imprisoning of my granny but I knew I was without blame. The upshot was that mother's plans to return to work were put on hold and life soon returned to normal.

To all intents and purposes life looked set fair, everything in the garden was rosy, literally, and to my mind there was no reason why we shouldn't live happily ever after. But life's not always like that, as I was to discover. One day, completely out of the blue, I found out that we were to move house. I don't know whether it was my mother or father who broke the news, perhaps it was both of them. I was three and a half and totally devastated, I remember shedding bitter tears. Despite my wailing and gnashing of teeth the inevitable came to pass and thus in 1953 the Thatcher family was installed in my mother's parents' house at 23 Bond's Hill. The new owner of Mill Cottage worked for Bibby's, a supplier of meal to farmers, and even today when I come across a reference to that company or see their logo a surge of resentment suddenly invades my thoughts. After all these years I still believe that Mill Cottage really encompassed what has now become known as 'The Good Life'.

THE WATERSIDE YEARS

Although I have strong memories of living at Bond's Hill, time has erased any recollection of our actual departure from Drumahoe or of setting up there. Number 23 was where my grandparents Minnie and Johnnie Bradley had lived since the end of the First World War. Strictly speaking the house belonged to Eaton's Bakery and was rented by my grandparents. Johnnie was a baker who had won international recognition for his breadmaking skills and had worked for Eaton's for some time. Eaton's was one of several bakeries which existed in the city; it was eventually forced to close by the rise of the multinationals but was then a flourishing local business with a fleet of delivery vans and a network of commercial outlets. The actual bakery was situated in Duke Street at the foot of Distillery Lane, no more than a couple of hundred yards from number 23.

A Little About the Bradley Family

My grandfather was born in the Lower Road, the street which runs below Francis Street and was at one time the main thoroughfare between the Bogside and the country out towards Bridgend and eventually Buncrana. His family had come into Derry from Carrigans sometime in the nineteenth century. He trained as a baker and was an Old Contemptible, one of those soldiers who enlisted at the very beginning of the war and were immediately despatched to Europe to face the might of the Kaiser's army. I recall him telling how they did their basic training at Finner Camp near Bundoran and were subsequently marched the sixty odd miles to Derry to entrain for England and thence France.

I only remember two things he shared with me about his wartime experiences. Firstly, how pleased he was that the army discovered his prowess as a baker. He had done time in the front line but this discovery meant that he was withdrawn from frontline duty and sent to the rear to bake bread to feed the troops. Had the army not been so quick to recognise his ability he would almost certainly have been amongst those who went over the top on the 1st July 1916 at the First Battle of the Somme as he was a member of the 36th Ulster Division. The upshot of that might have been that he was amongst the many casualties, possibly one of the thousands who lost their lives, and thus I would not have been. Secondly was his attitude to foreigners. At some stage he was posted to Egypt where the army employed local labour to do the more menial tasks. He found the native labourers to be somewhat lazy and thought the only encouragement they needed involved some kind of physical persuasion, more than likely with a big stick. I was slightly taken aback at this way of thinking but I suspect he was not terribly out of tune with his comrades and anyway he had by then been promoted to sergeant and was probably not too far out of line with how the military treated native labour throughout the empire.

On return from the war in 1919 he resumed his career as a baker and worked for many of the major local suppliers, including Brewster's from where he was 'headhunted' and finally became the foreman baker in Eaton's. Much later I discovered that on his return to civilian life he was invited by some local entrepreneurs to join them in setting up a new bakery. He refused on the grounds that they had elected to stay at home during the war and had used the opportunity to increase their wealth rather than serve their country. It was my mother who told me this story. I think that while she was proud of the stand which he had taken she was secretly a little regretful that she did not grow up as the daughter of a well-to-do businessman.

Bond's Hill was not the cul-de-sac which it is today. It was the main thoroughfare from Craigavon Bridge to the junction at Dale's Corner where you might continue straight ahead along Clooney Road in the direction of Limavady, or by turning right onto Glendermott Road continue up the hill towards Rossdowney and then on to Belfast. In the 1950s it was not a tremendously busy road but it was the main road out of town. It was still a cobbled street and our house was part of a terrace of about twenty dwellings which ranged along the right-hand side of the road as you went up towards the junction. Between the houses and the road there was a broad footpath which served as our playground.

Number 23 was a three-story terraced house. The front door led directly onto the pavement and immediately beside the front door was the back door, which led through a small archway to our backyard where there was a shed which held coal and other bits and pieces. The smallish backyard was dominated by the rear walls of the houses on Clooney Terrace which towered about thirty feet above. The ground floor consisted of a front room, a backroom where we mostly lived, with a parlour off it which served as the kitchen, and then the back door leading to the yard. On the first floor there was a very large room to the front with a bedroom to the rear. The bathroom was on the back return. There were three further bedrooms on the top floor. The large room on the first floor was occupied by Miss Steiner. She was an Austrian Jew who had fled her country before Hitler took power and become a lodger with my granny and grandfather. I later discovered that she was a talented artist who after the war went to New York where she earned a living from her paintings. She specialised in portraits. She left not long after we arrived, a question of space, I expect. Before she left she did a portrait of my mother, which is still in my possession.

We were quite a disparate lot in Bond's Hill: there were schoolteachers, an undertaker, a Head Constable, several business people, and although I was unaware of it at the time it was what we would now call a mixed area as regards religion and politics. Towards the bottom of the street there was Granny Pemble's shop, which was a bit of a magnet for me at the weekend when pocket money was issued. She kept a great selection of sweets still stored in big jars and sold by weight. She was very patient as she waited for children to eke out the best value possible for their threepenny bit or sixpence. Slightly further down, opposite the station, was Bridie's. Bridie ran a much more professional operation selling all sorts of provisions to the locals. Next door was The Bat and Ball Bar which remained a mystery to me for many a year and finally there was the Midland Cinema, one of six such establishments operating in the city at that time.

I am confident that I remember my mother and father heading off for a night's diversion at the Midland, my father snazzily dressed in a shirt and tie but for reasons known only to him shod in a pair of carpet slippers, much to my mother's chagrin. It was less than a hundred yards from our front door to the back stalls in the cinema. The Midland was also the location where I first recall being traumatised by a film. I had gone with my mother to see Devil Girl from Mars and an extraterrestrial had somehow managed to make one of the protagonists disappear with a simple glance from her devil girl eyes. She cast a withering glare at some unfortunate man and all that seemed to remain of him was a pair of spectacles lying on the ground. My mother later explained that this simply meant he had fled the scene so quickly that his glasses flew off and lay forlornly on the bare earth. Nevertheless, I remain wary of girls from Mars to this day.

As I said, the move from Drumahoe took place in early 1953 but little did I realise at the time the significance of the date. It was the year that Her Majesty Queen Elizabeth made her first visit to the city as a reigning monarch. The city pulled out all the stops for the event and I was taken along to witness this momentous visit. The Queen's itinerary was published well in advance so we knew that at some stage she would appear in Guildhall Square to inspect a guard of honour. Thus, we joined a mass of people in the square to welcome Her Majesty. Somewhere in a local newspaper archive there exists a photograph which shows me sitting on the footpath in front of the Northern Bank, a four-year-old me waving my Union Jack. Having dutifully inspected the Guard of Honour, Her Majesty made her way to Brook Park for a garden party at which local dignitaries would have an opportunity to glimpse her. We stood around at the entrance but were unsuccessful in catching any further sight of the Royal Party. My memory is that it was a very long day for very little reward. I doubt if the Queen even noticed my presence. I wonder if she had known it was my birthday would she have shot an admiring glance in my direction?

The real significance of 1953 was that I was getting near school age. Well, if truth be told maybe I wasn't. Being born in early July put me in an awkward situation: I was really too young to start school. My mother was having none of that – I was going to school if they would have me. The only dilemma was where to send me. The Waterside was blessed with a fine selection of schools for a nearly-four-year-old. There was the possibility of Ebrington which, I think, was still in May Street, Rossdowney located at the junction of Glendermott Road and Dungiven Road, and Clooney to be found at the top of Simpson's Brae, all very handy to Bond's Hill you would think. So, I was a little surprised when I found myself being led by my mother up the steps to The Londonderry Model Public Elementary School on the Northland Road, about half a mile from Bond's Hill as the crow flies but considerably further if you wished to stay dry and used the bridge to cross the river. No doubt to my mother this was perfectly logical. After all, hadn't she been a pupil there herself, as had all her brothers and sisters?

So it was that in September 1953 I began my education at The Model. It must have been one of the largest schools in town in its day. As preparation for the big day – and to be sure that I would be admitted even though I was technically 362 days too young to start – my mother took me to meet the headmaster Mr Clayton, who declared that he could see no impediment to my enrolment. So, that was that.

When I began, The Model still educated pupils up to the age of fifteen, so there I was, barely four, mixing with pupils who were itching to leave and start their working life. My first day is still clear in my mind. I was taken to school by my mother, presumably by bus as we did not possess a car at that stage. I was carefully led to the 'Baby Infants' classroom to be welcomed by my teacher. Mother had lovingly prepared something to eat for lunch and as an accompaniment, a drink of diluted orange in a clean cod-liver oil bottle with a screw top. I can still see her embarrassment when the teacher dismissed her drink with almost a sneer, explaining that that sort of thing was no longer necessary, that the government now provided milk for its little citizens. I was quite happy when day one concluded and I was collected by my mother and taken home. That is my sole recollection of my first day in education.

Physically the school was divided in three parts: Baby and Senior Infants had their own individual playground, separated by a low wall from the girls area which served Years Three to Seven, and finally for the remainder there was the boys' playground. I can't recall what the big people, the Years Ten to Fourteen – some of whom were undoubtedly already shaving and dying to be released so they might begin to earn a living – did in their free time. Each playground had its own toilet facilities which were pretty basic, no more than a lean-to shed. The boys had a few separate cubicles and there was a short stretch of plastered wall that served as a urinal which frequently became the site of high-peeing competitions. I had no flair for this work.

The only thing of note happened at the end of Baby Infants. We had been looking forward to becoming Senior Infants but the government intervened and we moved into P2, a new system which was designed to improve our education no end. I felt somewhat cheated. I was never to be a Senior Infant, I had had my seniority removed and was reduced to a number.

ON THE BUSES

It was around then, when I was aged five and a bit, that it was deemed safe that I should make my own way to school. This required me to walk up to Clooney Terrace, cross the main thoroughfare and embark on an Ulster Transport Authority (UTA) bus which would deliver me to the gates of The Model.

This was not a school bus but a public service vehicle used by one and all. No one appeared to think that a five-year-old travelling on public transport would be subject to any kind of risk and of course I was not the only one of my age to be using public transport. In those days buses still had a conductor whose duty was to issue tickets to the travelling public. The tickets were made of thick cardboard and if you bought a return you had the onerous task of keeping it safe all day for use on the return journey when it would be punched with a set of clippers. One Christmas I was delighted to get a bus conductor's outfit from Santa and spent ages issuing tickets to anyone entering our house. I was slightly miffed when The UTA bowed to progress and the old system was replaced by a newfangled machine which issued tickets from a roll of blank paper.

It was while travelling from school that I first experienced sectarianism. I had just alighted on Clooney Terrace and was looking forward to getting home when I was accosted by two boys who seemed to be more or less the same age as myself. They demanded to know whether I was a catholic or a protestant and were nonplussed to discover that I didn't know. Helpfully I suggested that if they waited I would run down home, ask my mother and report back with the answer. For all I know they may still be waiting. I still wonder which answer they were hoping for, whether they wanted to visit violence upon me or welcome me as a future comrade in arms. Despite this rather unwanted intrusion our street remained a tranquil haven with plenty of scope for play.

Bond's Hill was a cobbled street for most of the time I lived there and was never designed to take the amount of traffic it would eventually be required to absorb. It did however provide me with the opportunity to play a game which was common at the time – collecting car numbers. I would sit at the kerbside with my legs on the main carriageway, noting down car numbers as they drove past. It could take a couple of hours to fill one side of a page. Picture that nowadays. There would be a policeman at your door remonstrating with your parents for allowing their child to play in the traffic and even worse you'd be poisoned by fumes and at risk of being squashed by rushing cars. There'd probably also be a visit from Special Branch wondering what your interest in car number plates signified! At that time there were still horses and carts at work pulling their heavy loads over the cobbles too, their iron-shod wheels rattling as they moved slowly up and down the hill. I don't think they counted as they didn't carry a registration plate.

I also became quite friendly with a denizen of Melrose House, the old people's home at Dale's Corner, who seemed to spend his days tramping the streets before retiring for the night. To me he seemed always downcast, eyes firmly fixed on the ground. I discovered that he was constantly on the lookout for discarded cigarette butts which he broke up and refashioned into roll-ups. My mother swiftly dissuaded me from any further engagement with him.

Although the Waterside was very much a junior partner in our city, for those of us who lived there it provided more than enough entertainment. First of all, it was the location of two of our four railway stations. Railway travel was still enjoying tremendous popularity and we had the biggest and most important of the four stations at the bottom of our street. In the early fifties it was still a very busy hub both for passengers and freight. Regular as clockwork the station would spring to life at 6:30 am. A new arrival to the area might be roused from slumber by the sounds of engines getting up steam or the clank of trucks being shunted round the yard. Then there would be the sound of lorries bringing goods for transport to Belfast or collecting goods for distribution around the town and local villages. We residents never really heard any of this and dozed on, the noise having become part of the backdrop to our daily life.

I was a little frightened of the station. My father was often required as a serving member of the Royal Navy to take the train to wherever he was stationed at the time. We always went to the station to wave goodbye which I found rather difficult. My problem was compounded when, as we stood on the platform to say our farewell, the train would vent steam with a roaring hissing noise which would terrify me and frequently reduce me to tears. Even today, if we visit a heritage railway, that sound brings all those memories flooding back.

If you travelled down Bond's Hill past Watt's Distillery which by that time was just a bonded warehouse, you came to Duke Street which was a really busy commercial thoroughfare. One of the highlights for me was the blacksmith who worked in a yard accessed through an archway just off the main road. The blacksmith was happy to allow us to stand and watch as he replaced shoes on the enormous dray horses which still worked in the town. These huge animals stood peacefully as they were shod. First there was a hiss of steam as the iron shoe made contact with the foot, followed by the smell of burning hoof and the bang of the hammer as the shoe was secured with nails.

Just beside the railway station Wall's ice cream had a cold store from which they served local shops. My mother worked in there for a brief period, which was terrific as it meant that sometimes if a package got damaged we would be treated to an ice lolly or perhaps a 'Mivvi', a new invention combining an ice lolly and an ice cream. Further along, near where there was a kind of goose neck twist in the street, there lived an old lady who ran a shop where we bought comics. That was about as far as we would venture. Craigavon Bridge was never crossed unless on our way to school or accompanied by parents. Just behind us on Clooney Terrace there were several shops that my mother might frequent. There was the butcher's shop, known to us as 'Patsy's', where you could see the butcher cut the meat from the carcasses hanging from hooks at the rear of the shop. The floor was strewn with sawdust to absorb whatever fluids were emitted during the butchery process. Meat was still a luxury and a little was made to go a long way. I can still see my mother stuffing a fairly small piece of steak to stretch it sufficiently to feed half a dozen people. My memories of those days were of clean plates at the end of dinner – noses were not turned up at anything edible. The only other commercial establishments I frequented were Dale's chemists, where I would collect prescriptions for Granny, and Tillie's chip shop where we would sometimes get a fish supper as a treat.

In the other direction lay St. Columb's Park. To get to the park you walked up past Dale's Corner and made your way along the perimeter fence of HMS Sea Eagle, which housed the NATO Anti-Submarine Base. Unknown to me we were at the height of The Cold War and Derry had a key role to play in keeping the threat of communism at bay. My father eventually found employment there. The park seemed a long way off but was probably a five-minute walk. The wide, open space it provided became increasingly important after we got our first dog.

The acquisition of Tinkle, for so he was christened, was a story in itself. Mother and her elder sister Auntie Mamie had decided that a trip to Belfast was in order. I'm sure there was some serious reason for such an expedition, but it wasn't shared with me. This was a big deal – I'd never been to Belfast before. I'm not even sure I'd been very far out of the city at that stage of my life. The big day arrived at last. We met at our house and made our way down to the station, another first, we were going by train.

On arrival in Belfast the most important item on the agenda was food. We went to Woolworth's which in those days boasted a restaurant;

yet another first, a self-service restaurant where I could choose for myself! After our repast all four of us (Aunt Mamie had brought one of her sons) went off shopping. At least the ladies did, my cousin and I were dragged along as mere appendages. I didn't realise that shopping was such a pain; my legs were still rather short and my feet hurt quite dreadfully. However, my stoicism paid off. Eventually we found ourselves in Smithfield Market, one of Belfast's lost treasures. I believe the ladies were looking for bargains but as luck would have it, we found ourselves outside a row of pet shops. It must have been agreed beforehand because my mother would never have caved in so readily to my pleas; the upshot was we left with Tinkle, a small black and white mongrel pup with endearing markings over his ears. My cousin was allowed to get a guinea pig, which he christened Moses. We had a long walk back to the station but the journey home was made shorter as we played with our new pets.

Tinkle was to share our house for a number of years and together he and I explored the various nooks and crannies of St Columb's Park. It was a much less tended space than it is nowadays and allowed a young person's imagination to run freely, so Tinkle and I tracked Indians across the prairie and through the woods and set traps for grizzly bears before heading home for tea. Tinkle only embarrassed me once. He must have found a ball of string, which he proceeded to consume. As we all know, what goes in must come out, and out it came, not in a lump but as if from a string dispenser which you might find on the counter of a department store. It was just a little embarrassing to be walking along Clooney Road with your dog who was involuntarily trailing a couple of yards of string in his wake. After a few days and the judicious use of a pair of scissors the string finally ran out.

Who provided the entertainment for children in Bond's Hill? Ourselves, for the most part. There were a few people of a similar age to myself living in the area at the time. One in particular is clearly imprinted on my mind. Her father was the principal of a local primary school and she was wont to play school with us. She always played the role of teacher and would sit us in rows on her doorstep and begin to teach us. It came as no surprise that in later life she did indeed become a prominent schoolteacher and journalist.

There was only one boy in the street of my age as far as I can remember. His father was a head constable in the Royal Ulster Constabulary, a now-defunct rank which stood between sergeant and inspector. The only game I can clearly recall playing with him involved us throwing stones at one another in his backyard. The point of the game eludes me but at all costs you had to avoid being struck by a missile. Unfortunately, I failed and soon I was running up to our house with blood pumping out of a gash on my forehead. Immediately my mother realised that it was too much for a sticking plaster and I was whisked away to The City and County Hospital on Infirmary Road, looking down Clarendon Street. This was my first experience of a casualty department and within an hour or so I had two stitches inserted with a minimum of fuss and was sent on my way. I still have the scar, which as my hairline recedes has become more prominent.

A CIRCUS COMES TO TOWN

One event which caused a terrific stir locally was when Chipperfield's Circus announced their arrival in town. They were touring Ireland and were to spend a week in Derry, raising their big top on the Daisy Field on the periphery of the city on the Letterkenny Road.

This was a big deal: Chipperfield's was at the time one of the premier circuses in the world. It was long before using animals as acts became frowned upon and they had animals in abundance. We spent ages speculating what would happen if the lions and tigers were to escape. How many casualties would there be? Would they be able to cross the river and attack us in the Waterside? We were also concerned about the elephants. Why? To generate publicity for the circus there was to be a parade leaving from the railway station and wending its way across the bridge to The Daisy Field. The elephants were to be the stars of the parade. The town was rife with speculation: would the bridge be able to cope with the weight of twelve elephants? Would they be made to cross in small groups? The talk went on for weeks.

Needless to say, the parade crossed the bridge in complete safety. In later life I understood the power of publicity and suspect that it may have been generated by the showmen themselves. It was nonetheless a magnificent circus, one of the best I've ever attended. Later in life other circuses came and went. I remember the visits of Duffy's and the equally enjoyable Fossett's Circuses. They normally pitched their tent in either the Daisy Field or The Brandywell Showgrounds. I recall a visit to Duffy's at the Brandywell particularly well. During the course of the show the acrobats performed with a troupe of horses, doing all sorts of daredevil tricks as they galloped round the ring. After the performance members of the public were invited to have a go and the most daring of my cousins decided to have a shot at it. There was a prize of five pounds if you were able to stand on the horse's back for one turn round the ring. For safety's sake, each of the contestants had to wear a harness just in case they fell off. My cousin, who fancied himself a bit of a horseman, seemed to be doing rather well, but just as he had almost completed the circuit he came tumbling off. He returned to his seat rather discontentedly, explaining to us in a torrent of oaths how the circus people had jerked the rope to unbalance him and thus avoid having to pay out the reward.

The Twelfth of August celebrations created a bit of a stir as Bond's Hill was part of the official parade route every second year and was also a route used by bands and lodges making their way to the Cityside on alternate years. My father had somehow managed to keep a White Ensign, the flag of the Royal Navy, which he would proudly fly from our top window. We would watch from the windows of our front room on the first floor, usually joined by lots of friends and relatives who wanted to both enjoy the bands in some comfort and be supplied with endless cups of tea.

One day, without warning, my father summoned my mother and myself to the front door. There, parked at the kerb was a car. Nothing unusual in that, you might say, but it was our car. No doubt my mother and father had discussed it beforehand but there it stood, our first car, a black Standard 8. This would be my father's pride and joy and the means of escape from the city. Nothing gave my father more pleasure than to set off on a Sunday afternoon, head for Donegal and try to find a road he had never driven along before. As you might imagine, this sense of freedom gave rise to many interesting adventures. We might for example drive down a fairly rough track with grass growing in the middle of it and suddenly find ourselves at a beautiful unspoilt beach or. On the other hand, we might frequently arrive in the middle of a farmer's yard where we would have to do an about turn as the surprised farmer smiled in amusement.

My mother also enjoyed driving, having learned under the tutelage of her youngest brother. Whilst she became an accomplished driver in later life, she confided that while learning she found reversing impossible and so her practice drives mostly involved driving out the A6 towards Dungiven as far as Brackfield Bawn, where the road was briefly sufficiently wide to permit her to do a U-turn and head back to the city. The car gave us a freedom we had lacked before. It allowed us to get out as a family. Most weekends Mother would make a flask of tea and a few sandwiches and with Granny in the front seat we would set off at random, have our picnic at some deserted spot and be home in time for church at 6:00 pm.

All the while I was growing up, becoming aware that there was more to the world than me and other places beyond our wee city. My grandfather continued to bake in Eaton's. His day started around 4:00 am when he would rise, make tea for himself in a little saucepan reserved entirely for his use and walk down the street to his work, returning in the early afternoon. He took me to the bakery one day and I was overwhelmed by the sheer size of it all. I had been used to seeing flour carefully measured out in ounces in our kitchen, mostly by Granny. Here it was measured in hundred-weights and loaves rolled out of the oven by the hundred, still, at this time, unwrapped and plain. They were then loaded into bread vans to be delivered round the countryside and into local shops.

I never knew Granny to work although I think in her youth she had been in service. She used to tell me that at one stage she had been a teacher. I took that with a pinch of salt. Later in life I discovered that she had spent some of her childhood with relatives in Ray near Manorcunningham. She had been sent to the local school and as an older pupil she had indeed been assigned to teach some of the younger students, as was customary at the time. When she married, her job was to stay at home and look after the man she had married at the age of sixteen, and the children which she bore him. Her health began to deteriorate in the early fifties; she wasn't an elderly woman by any means but she had succumbed to arthritis and particularly rheumatism, which she bore with all the grace she could muster. The National Health Service was in its infancy then and research into the wide spectrum of ills afflicting mankind was only really getting underway. Granny's treatment for her ailments seems nowadays rather rudimentary: I remember Dr Hart coming to visit to give her gold injections. This wasn't cheap, about £2 a go from memory, which had to come out of an average wage of about £10 a week so they weren't administered too frequently.

Granny began to spend more and more of her time in an armchair in the living room. In a strange way, this turned to my advantage. Comics were very much my thing and we got loads of them: The Topper, The Dandy, and The Beano, to name a few. Unfortunately, I had not quite got the hang of reading so would happily perch on the arm of Granny's chair whilst she would read to me. I was in my element. One day I noticed that I was able to read silently to myself as Granny read out loud. Evidently I was a cunning little chap because I kept my newly acquired reading skills to myself, until one day I let the cat out of the bag by telling Granny she had skipped a line. She was pleased as punch with my progress but I had made work for myself, now I was the one who had to do the reading and she would do the listening.

My obvious love of the written word was encouraged by my mother who, when I was about seven years old, bought a collection of ten books – probably from a book club – and I set about reading them. My first effort was Robert Louis Stevenson's Treasure Island and I attempted to read at least a chapter a day. The ship 'The Hispaniola' caused my young brain a bit of a problem and it took ages to master the pronunciation. Every evening mother would quiz me on what I had read that day. I think she thought I might be a bit of a bluffer and was idly turning the pages without absorbing anything I had read. Next on the list was Children of the New Forest and A Christmas Carol, and finally a selection of Greek myths and legends which was quite daunting. Nearly seventy years later, I still have that set sitting safely on my shelves.

Life was proceeding quietly with the daily routine of bussing back and forward to school and weekends spent messing around the local area. I can't recall any summer holidays; I think that with the arrival of the car we would have gone to the seaside on good days and stayed at home on grey days. Our favourite location for a trip to the sea was Fahan, which still boasted a railway station with an occasional train puffing very slowly to Buncrana and equally slowly back to Derry. In the summer it sometimes happened that there would be an outing to Portrush. Rather to my surprise, Granda would go on these outings from time to time. We would pull up in the car park at Ramore Head and without a word he would get out of the car and set off towards the putting green which was part of the recreation grounds. Not once did he invite us to play a round with him. He would then take a leisurely stroll around the headland and arrive back at the car, his day complete. No one ever questioned this rather eccentric behaviour.

Life had taken on a rather predictable, almost soporific quality: school, holidays, an unchanging humdrum of daily life. However, unbeknownst to me, big changes were afoot. Eaton's were expanding, necessitating a move to a new bakery situated on the Strand Road on the opposite side of the river. We were on the move once more. This time I was more prepared. There was a hint of sadness mixed with some apprehension, but mostly a sense of expectation.

It had been decided that the Thatchers would buy a house as Eaton's had nothing suitable to rent. One day I was taken to see our proposed new dwelling. We got out of the car in front of number three Nicholson Terrace, a short street off Academy Road. It was a terraced house three storeys tall but it was in a terrible state. Its previous owner had been a very old lady who had not lived in it for a number of years. Facilities were minimal: there was no indoor toilet and the kitchen consisted of an ancient range and a jaw-box sink. I'm sure my mother was horrified but my father had faith. It cost eight hundred pounds, quite an investment at the time. Since we had planned ahead there was no rush to move in.

Builders were engaged and the renovation work began. The first project was the addition of a two-storey rear extension which would give us a new kitchen with a toilet and bathroom above. In the backyard a garage was created and the outhouses put into a good state of repair. When that was complete the entire house was decorated, which transformed the dark, soot-stained interior into a bright, airy, five-bedroomed house into which we moved in the summer of 1956. I had just turned seven.

THE CITYSIDE

The move took place with the minimum of fuss and the family quickly settled into our new home. On the ground floor we had the 'good room' next to the sitting room and the kitchen in the new extension. The 'good room' was only to be used on special occasions, for example when the minister came to visit or important relatives had to be impressed.

Like most families, the kitchen was where most of the day-to-day living took place. There was a range which burnt this newfangled anthracite stuff and a gas cooker where a teapot seemed to perpetually dispense a dark brew that gathered strength as the day progressed. The first floor accommodated Johnnie and Minnie and my mother and father and there were three bedrooms on the top floor, one of which was entirely mine. Granny's illness continued to worsen and every day was a trial for her, particularly getting downstairs in the morning and back to bed at night, but she persevered. Most of her day she spent in an armchair in the sitting room from whence she had a great view of all the comings and goings in the backyard. Johnnie continued to work as usual, still rising at 4:00 am to set off to his daily labours.

An unforeseen consequence of our move to the Cityside was that suddenly I was so much closer to school. The side entrance on Academy Road was no more than one hundred yards from my bedroom door. No longer would I have to rise early rain hail or snow to catch a bus across town. I could stroll slowly down at 8:30 am and be sure to be on time.

When we transferred from P2 to P3, we physically moved upstairs to the first floor. My clearest memory of P3 is of raffia mats: we seemed to spend an inordinate amount of time making little placemats which consisted of a disc of cardboard around which we wound lengths of raffia dyed in various bright colours. I was quite pleased as for once I was able to achieve a finished product that looked fairly presentable. When we graduated to painting, things went badly awry. I had no grasp of perspective or use of colour. I don't believe I ever produced anything that I would have been pleased to take home to show my mother. Other people were forever carting things off for doting mammies and daddies to admire.

The bane of my existence in P3 was learning to write with an ink pen. There were several varieties of nibs available and the nib favoured by the school just had to differ from the one I had been practising with at home. We used copy books where the task was to replicate the sentence set out in perfect form on the line above. No matter how diligent I was I found the nib impossible to master and continually produced a line of scratches and blotches. The teacher was at her wits' end, nothing she tried could help me improve. My parents asked that I might be allowed to use my own pen from home. Some chance! Luckily, Mr Biro would come to my aid before too long. I just thanked my lucky stars I hadn't been born left-handed as those who had were still subjected to all kinds of remedies, some quite brutal, to encourage them to write with the right hand.

When I reached the dizzy heights of P6 our classes took place at the opposite end of the building. This had a much more agreeable aspect as the windows looked out on the City and County Hospital, which was set in rather pleasing grounds with mature trees and lots of rhododendron bushes. The changing nature of the trees allowed us to mark the seasons of the year and particularly the approach of the summer holidays. We watched out for the leaves turning gold in autumn and the falling of the helicopter seeds from the sycamore trees, the stark outline of the branches in the winter sun followed by the birds starting to build their nests and then the fresh buds of spring suggesting holidays were not far off. Another vista from our classroom was the enormous set of windows to the side of the hospital building just across the avenue. We were told that these windows allowed the light into the operating theatre and we often speculated on what gruesome activities might be taking place just a few yards from our comfortable classroom. Maybe some poor soul was losing a limb or expiring on the operating table.

There was still a hint of military discipline in the way the school functioned; I suppose the war was not long over and some of the staff may have been active participants in the conflict. One manifestation of this rigorous regimentation was how the school day ended. When the final bell rang we were expected to congregate on the driveway in front of the school and as soon as we were neatly formed into rows by class, we were marched to the bottom of the drive where we were brought to attention and dismissed. Since the drive measured no more than seventy or eighty yards this seemed a little pointless but I supposed it prevented a howling mob of children rushing onto the main road and into the oncoming traffic. I think of the moment we marched off when I still get slightly confused between left and right. I imagine myself formed up on the driveway and know that my left is the side closest to the school building.

One other outworking of the lingering remnants of a military past revolved around Empire Day. I may be one of the few remaining who recall celebrating this now defunct ceremony. The final one took place in 1958, before it was briefly replaced by Commonwealth Day. I clearly recollect the entire school going on parade on the playground in front of the headmaster's house. We lined up in rows facing the flagpole where the Union Flag was raised high and no doubt we sang patriotic songs such as 'Rule Britannia', which we had rehearsed endlessly in class, finishing with the National Anthem. At the time I had no idea what it was all about; for us it was a diversion and some time out of the classroom. Many years later when visiting the Model School, I was astonished and delighted to find a photograph of that day on display in the foyer. I was able to pick out my eight-year-old self standing proudly to attention with my classmates. I don't think anyone amongst the current staff realised the significance of the photograph, it was merely a random picture of the school in days gone by. It's also astonishing to think that as we stood proudly at attention saluting the flag, the sun was beginning to set on that empire upon which it was once said the sun never set.

By this stage The Model had lost its twelve-to-fifteen-year-olds to the newly constructed secondary intermediate schools of Templemore and Clondermot, so we as P7 pupils had reached the pinnacle of our time in primary school and were accorded certain privileges as befitted our age and status. One of these so-called privileges was to help the caretaker first thing in the morning, a task which required some of us to be in school perhaps half an hour before anybody else. One of the caretaker's duties was to distribute the milk, which was delivered in crates to the back door. We then had to transfer the appropriate number of crates to the door of each classroom, using a trolley to move them from one end of the school to the other. This was fairly easy for the ground-floor classrooms but to get to the first floor the crates had to be manhandled up two flights of stairs and put on another trolley for delivery. We undertook these tasks willingly and voluntarily. We were ten years old and we loved it, we were becoming big boys.

On our journey through primary school we encountered teachers of all sorts. In the early years we were mostly taught by women. Some of them I remember with great fondness, others with a certain sense of apprehension. As we progressed we encountered more male teachers and in our final two years they were exclusively male. My P7 teacher was a former combatant in the Second World War and would regale us with tales of his time in the desert fighting Rommel, but only if he was in a good mood, which wasn't too often. Most days he ruled us with a rod of iron, or rather a cane of bamboo. He was one of the 'Derry Boys', who served in the 9th Anti-Aircraft Regiment Royal Artillery, made up mostly of young men from the city who on the outbreak of hostilities became full-time soldiers under the command of Sir Basil McFarland. His tales of life in the desert were no doubt enhanced to impress us youngsters, for whom stories of derring-do were fresh in our minds and kept alive by the characters we encountered in the comics we read each week.

P7 of course was the year of 'The Qually', the entrance test for secondary school and the bane of every eleven-year-old in the country. At the time we were made to feel that the rest of our life depended on success in this examination. Some parents took a fairly sanguine view and attempted to maintain a relaxed attitude to the whole thing, others applied quite severe pressure on their sons and daughters. I never got the impression that I was under any real pressure; the underlying feeling was that it would be better to pass but failure could be managed. Throughout P7 a great deal of time was devoted to preparation for the tests and teaching of the rest of the curriculum took a bit of a back seat. What did we learn beyond the test papers? Well, we were taught about the rivers, lakes, mountains, and towns of Ireland and what was produced where. If pushed, I can still bring to mind some of those facts. We also briefly studied the geography of England but I don't think we ventured into history at all.

Strangely we also learned about South Africa, its towns and cities and what they produced. Famously I put my hand up in response to a question as to what the principal product of the town of Kimberly might be. When I gave my answer I was rather pleased with myself and was taken aback when the whole class burst into laughter. 'Biscuits', I had confidently announced, confusing a famous product of the Jacob's Biscuit Company with the rather more valuable diamonds mined in the South African town. Inexplicably the teacher decided to spare the rod on that occasion, perhaps my embarrassment was sufficient punishment. Another of our teachers had gone to Japan during the summer holidays. On his return he talked to us about his experiences and had brought back some Japanese treats for our delectation. Some of my classmates were sufficiently bold as to try the insects dipped in chocolate which he offered for our delectation. My palate, I'm afraid, did not stretch to such exotic morsels.

BACK TO THE ELEVEN-PLUS

We seemed to spend endless amounts of time going through practice papers, even going to the lengths of putting all the entrants into the school assembly hall to try and recreate test conditions. We learned tricks and techniques to deal with the questions.

Every year, candidates were presented with a question on time. A favourite was to tell the correct time from a clock portrayed as a mirror image. We quickly learned that all you needed to do was turn the page and look at it from the other side. No doubt that tested some kind of intelligence. For some who were fortunate to have parents who could afford to invest in us, our teacher ran a crammer session once a week after school, where we did even more practice questions and tried to master techniques which would make the test less onerous. It cost half a crown; I can still see them piled up on the teacher's desk and I felt obliged to make the most of it because I'm sure it was money that was required elsewhere in the household budget.

When the big day finally arrived, my fellow competitors and I – for competition it was – made our way to the newly constructed Templemore Intermediate School to sit the test. I had a brand-new pencil case filled with freshly sharpened pencils, an ink rubber, a pencil rubber, and a variety of writing implements. I certainly wasn't going to fail for lack of equipment. We sat in our well-spaced ranks and before we knew it, it was all over and we had the rest of the day off. This was repeated about two weeks later and the whole process was put to the back of our minds. School took a turn for the better after that and lessons had a much more leisurely feel to them. Suddenly more sport became available to us and we played cricket and football on the field behind the school.

Living so close to the school had other advantages. For example, at lunchtime I could be sitting having a nice warm meal in our kitchen whilst my fellows had to make do with packed lunches. It also gave me a certain local knowledge which meant I could be entrusted with running errands for the teacher. I would frequently be dispatched to buy twenty Gallagher's Blues in the local All Cash Stores for our teacher, who from time to time could not contain his craving and would smoke a sneaky cigarette whilst leaning out of the classroom window. I was also sent to McLaughlin's shop in William Street to buy a cane. I was a little fearful as I knew that previously a teacher had sent a pupil to buy a rod for his own caning; a 'rod for his own back', so to speak. I knew I had done nothing wrong but was still relieved when, on my return, the cane was safely locked away in a cupboard.

Conker season began the school year and the chestnut trees which lined the school drive provided some champion material. Others foraged further afield to discover potential winners. There were fine trees lining Duncreggan Road in front of The Londonderry High School but others went even further abroad to secure a super conker. There was rumoured to be a fine stand of chestnut trees at Birdstown, not far from Bridgend, but that was miles beyond my reach. People went to great lengths to improve the quality of their weapon; some swore that time in a warm oven made them more hardy, others soaked them in brine for a few days. Whatever I did, nothing seemed to improve my luck. I can still see myself holding an empty piece of string with my chestnut in pieces at my feet.

When the weather turned chilly it allowed the possibility of making slides in the icy playgrounds. These were frowned upon by school staff and you had to be in early in the morning to get sliding. Whilst I enjoyed having a go I was always a bit timid and the usual outcome was a grazed elbow or a skinned knee. Marbles was a year-round activity and could be played anywhere where there was an indentation in the ground to serve as the goal to get your marble into. It was a game with a huge array of rules, most of which required you to shout out louder and more quickly than your opponent. 'High Heights' required you to play your marble from shoulder height but I no longer have an inkling of what 'Full follies' meant. Local rules also came into play so before you started you needed a good grounding in what variations were in force at the time. Some boys amassed huge bagfuls of multicoloured 'marlies' won from less able opposition; my cache remained pitifully small.

Television entered our lives towards the end of the fifties. We had watched patiently as the enormous mast was erected on Sheriff's Mountain to diffuse programmes from the BBC across Derry and parts of Limavady. The Thatchers had not the means to buy a television set but one of our near neighbours did, so after school a group of young lads would congregate in the front room to watch the television. There might have been up to a dozen small boys squeezed into a not-overly-large sitting room. At first, we spent most of our time watching the television set. Broadcasting had not officially begun and often all we might see were some intermittent glimpses of the test card but even that was sufficient to hold us in its thrall. Eventually programmes became regularised and we sat contentedly watching whatever the BBC thought appropriate for children at that time. The first programme I ever saw from beginning to end was Bengi the Boxer Puppy. The whole proceedings would come to a very abrupt ending when my friend's father returned from work. He was a man who liked children to be neither seen nor heard, so the noise of his car drawing up outside the house prompted a rapid exit and a scattering of boys to the four winds.

THE FAMILY HOME

Number Three Nicholson rapidly became the hub of the Bradley clan and rarely a day went by without some member of the family dropping in. The Bradleys had subdivided into Bradleys, Fosters, and Thatchers, with an occasional sprinkling of Dohertys and Nelis's who were slightly more distant relatives.

I seemed to have any amount of 'second cousins once removed'. The Bradleys were difficult to pin down. Uncle Bob, the eldest son and he who had invited my father home for Christmas all those years ago, had married an Englishwoman, Aunt Joan. They were more or less domiciled in England, and apart from a few years when he was stationed at Killylane overlooking Lough Foyle and living in Downhill and latterly at Campsie, we didn't see too much of them. Nevertheless, this side of the family were frequent visitors to Nicholson during their sojourn at Campsie and continued to visit on an almost annual basis after their return to England. My three female cousins from this branch of the family spent some time as boarders at Londonderry High School, which they continue to recall with some affection.

My Uncle Eric and his family spent a significant part of my childhood abroad. Uncle Eric had just managed to catch the last few months of World War Two. He had served as a merchant seaman on the Atlantic convoys, judiciously arranging to indulge his passion for music by taking in some concerts by the greats of the twentieth century whilst docked in New York. Uncle Eric was the 'coolest' member of the family and a great jazz aficionado, who regaled us with tales of the artists he had seen all those years ago. After the war he joined the army and spent some time in both Hong Kong and Germany before settling finally in Northern Ireland. Uncle Jack had also joined the navy and spent the war at sea, often on aircraft carriers fighting the Japanese in the Pacific. When the war was over he spent a brief period in Australia before he also returned to Derry. He was stationed at Eglinton where the navy still maintained an airborne presence. His children were frequent visitors to Granny, Granda, Uncle John and Aunt Gladys. Aunt Mamie was an equally frequent visitor but life on the farm at Creevagh could be hectic, what with men to feed and cows to milk, and that occupied her most of the time.

Number Three certainly was a very busy location; few days would pass without the sound of the latch on the back gate opening, alerting us to the imminent arrival of one visitor or another. For me it also acted as an early warning system, as some guests were more welcome than others and the noise of the latch gave me the option of whether to stay around or make a swift escape to my room. The essential criteria for staying around were one: was there the prospect of buns or pastries being produced and two, what were the chances of a sly sixpence or shilling being slipped into my hand as farewells were exchanged? Most visitors were relatives but it was often difficult for me to unravel the labyrinthine connections which glued the family together. To this day I fail to understand the link connecting first cousins twice removed!

SCHOOL AND BEYOND

Having moved house without having to move school put me at a great advantage because I had a readymade circle of acquaintances, though given that there were several other primary schools in the area there were lots more potential friends to make.

First, let me describe the locality. I lived in Nicholson Terrace, named after the developer rather than the Nicholson of Indian fame or infamy, depending on your point of view. It was a street of about twenty dwellings occupied by a disparate bunch of people, ranging from schoolteachers to policemen, shopkeepers, and a variety of civil servants. The street abutted Nicholson Square and immediately behind were De Burgh Terrace and Square with further along Stewart's Terrace. De Moleyn Terrace was a stretch of six new houses which formed part of the much longer De Burgh Terrace. Brooke Park, which could be accessed through a side entrance from Stewart's Terrace, would prove to be a major feature in our play.

One of the most notable influences on my life, which appeared almost from nowhere, was church. When we lived in the Waterside, church attendance was very much a sporadic activity. In Bond's Hill we lived less than one hundred yards from what ought to have been our local parish church, All Saints Clooney, yet I have no recollection of having attended a service there. I have one distant memory of going to church at Glendermott Parish Church and being so discontented that I spent most of the service playing underneath the pew. Christ Church was to be different. It had been the family church when the Bradleys lived on the Cityside; I had been baptised there, my parents had been married there, Christ Church had held the Bradley and now Thatcher family in its firm embrace, as I was about to discover.

ME, A CHOIRBOY?

At some stage after our move my mother decided that I was to learn something about music, and what better way than to become a choirboy? The obvious choice was Christ Church – after all, it was free.

She made inquiries and sure enough I was enrolled as a Probationer in Christ Church choir. There may have been some kind of audition but whether there was or wasn't, I was soon appearing in my red robe and a ruff round my neck every Sunday for Matins and Evening Prayer and Wednesday Evensong in the choir stall reserved for probationers, just behind the real choir. There was also choir practice every Friday evening, so singing occupied quite a chunk of my life over the next five or six years.

I also became a member of the Second Londonderry Cub Pack, also attached to Christ Church, and once a week swore to do my duty to God, the Queen, and of course the public at large. Being a Cub was great 'craic'. It gave wee boys an opportunity to wreck and tear in the Craig Memorial Hall, the church hall, once a week. We were taught a wide variety of skills: how to tie knots, light fires, cook, map read, and possibly most important of all, to behave in a civilised manner. Instruction in the latter required a great deal of patience from our leaders.

Much more later of choirs and Cubs. What else was there locally to divert a young lad? Fortunately, it was still an era when children would play on the streets without fear, and that is what we did. The area was populated by families with young children and we were encouraged to mingle and play street games together. There were enough boys to gather up a group to play football on the street, often against the gable wall of someone's house. We also played handball or tennis, once again against a gable wall. I don't know how the owners of these houses put up with us, indeed some of them didn't and as we were chased away we were told in no uncertain terms what fate awaited us if we came back. We were lucky; we had the freedom of the area and we lived in a network of streets without much traffic, besides which the ownership of cars was not that common in the 1950s.

BROOKE PARK

Our boundaries were pretty clear cut and we seldom ventured beyond them. We lived life between the Academy Road and the far wall of Brooke Park. We seldom ventured further up Academy Road than the old Foyle College building or further down than Northland Road.

The park was an amazing asset. It had a playground right at the very top beside Park Avenue. There we had access to a variety of swings, roundabouts and slides, just perfect for growing boys. There were tennis courts and a bowling green, both frequented by grown-ups and of no interest to us though, as we got older, we might have cast a glance at the tennis players, particularly the females. As you progressed further down the park there were areas of open parkland which we could transform into Wembley Stadium with the judicious placement of a few jumpers for goalposts. Then came the more formal part of the park, where gardeners tended to beautiful rose beds and wonderfully planted parterres, all under the eagle eye of the park rangers who patrolled ceaselessly and put the fear of God into miscreant youths. The shrill blast of a whistle was enough to send a hoard of errant youths diving for cover.

Here too was Gwyn's Institute, which once provided succour for destitute children before becoming the municipal museum and finally the City Library. Adjacent to the library was the ornamental pond with its water lilies and, if you were lucky enough to spot them, a selection of fish which we thought were goldfish but were more likely carp. There was a stretch of rhododendron bushes which ran from the side entrance at Stewart's Terrace to the main gate on Infirmary Road. They came out from the wall to the main path, a breadth of about ten yards or so, and provided an ideal ground for our adventures. One day we could be fighting the Japanese in the thickest jungles in the Pacific, the next we would be ambushing Red Indians or driving herds of cattle across the plains of North America. All this came to a sudden stop when we heard rumours of a boy being molested in those very bushes. We soon got over that and the park continued to provide an ideal backdrop for our many and varied activities.

It wasn't long before the library began to ensnare me. The building itself was not the most alluring to our young eyes; it looked grey and grim and a little foreboding. Nonetheless, I was soon drawn to the library, which occupied one half of the ground floor with the entrance around the corner at the far side of the park. My grandfather was a great reader, an avid consumer of Westerns, and I believe it may have been he who originally introduced me to the library and stood guarantor for my membership. The library itself was rather old-fashioned and certainly not purpose built; at best it was a space for storing books as neatly as possible. The Children's Section was tucked away in a small room to one side of the main library. Children were allowed to choose two books. I would lean towards a Biggles book by W.G. Johns and a Billy Bunter story by Frank Richards, perhaps. I couldn't wait to get home and get stuck into them. I remember lying in bed reading until I got them both finished.

Next day after school I was back up to the library to swap them for my next two. The librarian gave me a quizzical look but I assured him I was a quick reader. Little did I know at the time that some years later I would be working in the library, dealing with children just like myself. I had other experiences during my spell in the library – I was working the night we discovered incendiary devices placed in the books. In our naivety my colleague and I simply searched through the books, found the devices and threw them into a bin; we didn't even alert the few customers who were in the library at the time. Next day there was hell to pay: I was given a fool's pardon as I had only just started working for the library but my colleague was not so fortunate. It was also during my time that the whole building was set alight, leading ultimately to its demolition. That's a story for another day.

The building had also at one time housed the City's Museum and I can clearly recall seeing the coach which once belonged to the Knox family of Prehen sitting forlornly in a shed to the rear of the building. There were also random stuffed animals in glass cases and other one-time exhibits scattered round the area. The upper storey housed the offices of local government departments of the day, for example the main office of the local education department was situated in Brook Park. I often wonder what became of all the various, probably quite valuable, exhibits which were once stored there.

The Library, as we called it, was fronted by quite a grand esplanade adorned with a few antique cannon. I recall band concerts taking place there on summer's evenings. The town had quite a number of brass and silver bands and even for us 'weans' it was a welcome diversion to sit and listen for a while before setting off on some more youthful pursuit.

OTHER PURSUITS

Immediately behind Nicholson Square and De Moleyn Terrace there was a patch of wasteland, probably about an acre, which provided even more space for our adventures. It was too rough for sporting activities but was another location for cowboys and Indians, war games, and other outrageous events.

It was also the site where we constructed our Easter hut. This was a tradition which stretched across the city. Usually around the start of March, little boys around the town might be seen carrying all kinds of rudimentary digging implements, hellbent on the construction of these dens. Frequently they were built on exactly the same location year after year, which allowed for grander and grander structures, some of them extending to two or even three-roomed temporary underground dwellings. Our hut was dug about four feet into the ground and had a roof of old abandoned timbers covered with sacking and sods. Inside it was pretty waterproof and in the wall it had a kind of fireplace which served both as a heat source and a cooking area where we fried sausages and the occasional egg, a cuisine of questionable quality. When Easter was over the hut was abandoned for another year.

This area was hidden from the public gaze and probably for that reason it was where we gathered to indulge our smoking habit. It was where I took my first drag on an illicit cigarette, a Gallagher's Blue more than likely acquired by nefarious means, perhaps pilfered from a packet casually left lying around our house. It became a habit which took more than twenty years to break.

It was in this location that we built our one and only 'Twelfth' bonfire. We were not a sectarian bunch, it was a 'one off' occasioned by the discovery of some offcuts of timber abandoned by a builder and attended by local children out for a bit of random entertainment. The memory of it has never left me. Carried away by the notion of what was expected, rather than what I really thought, I felt compelled to express some kind of fervour appropriate to the occasion and was moved to exclaim: 'To hell with King William and God save the Pope'. This rather startled my neighbour Frances standing beside me who, being a member of the congregation of Saint Eugene's Cathedral, was not anticipating such an affirmation of support for His Holiness from a member of The Church of Ireland. Thankfully no one noticed my double-edged foolishness and henceforth I have been more circumspect in public declarations of any sort. A lesson well learnt.

Another pastime which could go on for hours was a game of Hide and Seek, which we called a 'Wide Game'. You defined the area where the game would take place and how long it was to last, then divided into hunters and hunted, with the latter having a few minutes to get away before the hunt began. The winner was the last person to be discovered. The possibilities were enormous as you could hide in someone's garden, in a garage, or up a back lane. One of my favourite spots was in a clump of high-standing flowers round the back of somebody's house. Eventually people got to know your hideouts and might have ignored you just for a laugh. I remember having hidden undiscovered for ages when suddenly the Angelus rang at 9:00 pm, marking the end of the game and time to go home. The next day I found out that people knew exactly where I was but had decided to just leave me there until home time. It wouldn't be the last time I was ignored.

After summer holidays the next big thing to look forward to would be Halloween, or more precisely, fireworks. Bangers would begin to appear in shops towards the end of September and we would scout around to see who was selling what and if there were bargains to be had. It must be remembered that there was no regulation of fireworks at that time, so if you had the money you could buy whatever took your fancy. Nearly every corner shop would stock bangers of some kind and they were generally one old penny each. A superior, more powerful device could be had for two pence. We generally went for quantity over quality and if we wanted a bigger bang we would tie a few together. Thinking back, we were incredibly thoughtless in our use of these fireworks. It was an act of some bravado to hold these explosives at arm's length until they burst asunder. On one occasion I witnessed a banger being slipped surreptitiously into a boy's hip pocket. Somehow he managed to extricate it in time but had to go home and explain a singed pair of jeans to his mother. We might also have thrown them into people's gardens or into porches – we were lucky we weren't taken aside and given good hiding.

Halloween itself was a more family-orientated time. As October 31st approached, excitement would mount. We were lucky we were born before the awful 'Trick or Treat' phenomenon arrived. We were still linked to the old Celtic-inspired festival of Samhain when we dressed up and lit bonfires to ward off evil spirits. We certainly did not go around neighbours' houses in the hope of being given sweets. The expectation was that any feasting that we might indulge in would be on apples or nuts. Halloween also meant proper fireworks, something slightly more upmarket than bangers and supervised by grown-ups. Sky Rockets, Catherine Wheels and Roman Candles would be the order of the day, set off by adults who took great pleasure in organising their display. My cousins tell me that the introduction of the family firework display was due to the interest shown by my father. Our Halloween usually took place on my uncle's farm at Sheriff's Mountain. It would begin with games like ducking for apples in the kitchen, which frequently left the participants soaking wet. At some point Auntie Mamie would produce a couple of apple tarts which we devoured with lashings of fresh cream. When it was dark enough, we went outside to watch the fireworks and then the bonfire was lit. One of the highlights was to watch bonfires on neighbouring farms light up in turn. I think there was a kind of order to their lighting which reflected perhaps a lingering memory of days gone by when they might have been lit as a kind of distress signal.

As Halloween faded from our memory, we began to think of the possibility of snow and sleighing. For the most part we had little time to indulge our passion for snowballing or sledging. Snow came at night, lay for a few hours, and was gone. Snowballs might only be thrown in that brief period before school began and there was never a decent enough fall to warrant getting the sledge out. The winter of 1962 – 63 changed all that. It snowed shortly after Christmas and it seemed to last forever. The corporation policy seemed to consist of sending men round in open lorries, with a man on the back shovelling grit onto the road; pavements were usually left untreated. When conditions were right, we sleighed on Nicholson Square and Stewart's Terrace. The latter was a slightly longer run but required a rather brisk stop at its conclusion to avoid being precipitated over the low wall and into the Model School football pitch below. More daring people might have gone to Lawrence Hill, which was steeper and longer but had the danger of sleighing out into the traffic on Strand Road. Mind you, at that time a car might have passed every three or four minutes. Even more adventurous people made their way to Todd's Hill, now known as Groarty Road, which had a run of about a mile from the top down to Northland Road at the bottom. To me it seemed a very long walk to make your way back to the top for a second go. I suspect that a combination of global warming and excess traffic means the thrill of a good run on a sledge will never be available to young people again, unless they choose to become Olympians.

CHRISTMAS

Christmas was a big deal for most families, especially if Santa was expected to work his magic. We always had a visit from Santa when we lived in Bond's Hill and he still managed to find us when we moved to Nicholson Terrace. Typically, Christmas morning began with discovery of what Santa had put in your Christmas stocking, then it was downstairs to see what had been left under the tree.

Bond's Hill was a focal point for the whole family and on Christmas afternoon as many of the extended family as were available would gather for the festivities. For some reason we were twice blessed as Santa would pay us a special visit during the course of the afternoon. I was curious to know why Santa treated our family in particular to a double visit. Anyway, there was Santa seated on our armchair, surrounded with even more presents with his long beard and his 'Ho-ho-ho's'. Being curious, I was poking around at Santa's feet looking at the presents when suddenly, as Santa crossed his legs, I caught a glimpse of the long pink bloomers he seemed to be wearing. At the time I said nothing – Santa wasn't someone you wanted to upset – but later it occurred to me that Granny never seemed to be in the room at the same time as Santa.

The second Christmas story involves trains. My father was always fascinated by trains, especially those of the Great Western Railway Company which had of course been subsumed into British Rail at the time of nationalisation. He had imbued me with a liking for trains and between us we had bought a small Hornby train set. When I say 'between us', of course I mean he bought it, probably more for himself than me. We had spare room in the attic and he had set up the track and screwed it onto a board so it could be played with at the drop of a hat. Anyway, both of us were getting great fun out of running the coaches round and round the track but I could sense that he had ambitions. Nothing was said but I knew that something was afoot. It was near

Christmas but I had made no declaration as yet as to what I might like from Santa. Hints were dropped and shortly I was writing to request some additional rolling stock for the train set. The letter was sent and I thought no more of it; Santa had always managed to come up trumps in the past so I had no qualms he would be able to deliver again this year.

One day, for no sensible reason, I was in the 'good room', the one only used when the clergy arrived or for special family gatherings involving relatives from further afield. I was rummaging around and suddenly spotted beneath the settee several packages wrapped in newspapers. In our house it wasn't unusual to discover family 'heirlooms' which had been wrapped up and forgotten but this was a bit different. I pulled out one of the packages and suddenly realised my error: I had uncovered Santa. I pulled out several more packages and discovered the beginnings of a serious Hornby train set. Hastily I rewrapped them and returned them to their hiding place. Nothing was ever said and I feigned great delight on Christmas morning, but I just knew I was fooling no one, not even myself.

HURRICANE DEBBIE

The most significant meteorological event of my life was Hurricane Debbie, which arrived early in September 1961. Debbie came roaring up the west coast of Ireland having originated somewhere in West Africa. It was pretty fierce. We had some prior warning but I don't believe we were advised to stay indoors or take any particular precautions.

The All Cash Stores, our local corner shop, had quite an extensive plate glass window which managed to survive the force of the huge gusts, unlike the quite recently completed Clondermot Secondary School, which had its roof ripped off and was closed for months. My most vivid memory of the storm is of being out in the street watching slates being torn from roofs and floating on the wind, until they crashed and shattered on the footpath. Why we were allowed out of the house I do not know. I find it equally unbelievable that I could stand facing the wind, jump into the air, and be blown back several feet by its force. It would take something considerably stronger to move me even a few inches nowadays.

The aforementioned All Cash Stores on the corner of Academy Road and De Burgh Terrace played a fairly significant part in our early lives. It was the go-to shop before we were overwhelmed by the arrival of supermarkets. It sold almost everything that the local family required and operated a system where you could buy things on tick and square your bill at the end of the week. It was also possible to do the equivalent of an online order. You wrote your order in a little red book which was unique to you, handed it over the counter, and later that day your order would be delivered to your door by a young man on a message bike. The process when re-invented by supermarkets many decades later required a man and a van to operate it. Every branch in the chain employed a message boy whose responsibility it was to deliver these orders.

Generally, it was a boy who had just left school, though sometimes it was somebody who had not yet finished school but was happy to do the rounds after completing his learning for the day and on Saturdays.

In my early teenage years The All Cash Store served as a kind of clubhouse for myself and a couple of my pals. It had two storerooms, one pretty dry and warm and the other more of a garage, with a large door that opened for deliveries. Twice a week there would be a delivery of potatoes in hundredweight bags. In return for being allowed to sit in the back storeroom we would weigh out these potatoes into quarter and half-stone bags. When we eventually got experienced enough, we were promoted to weighing out flour from ten-stone bags into half-pound and one-pound bags. This was a much more delicate activity and the bags required a very tricky method of closing off the top, not to be undertaken lightly. We got no reward for this other than to be allowed to sit in the store after school and an occasional bun which had passed its best.

CHANGES AFOOT

As the fifties drew to a close, so did my time at primary school. Many weeks after sitting the Eleven-plus, the dreaded day arrived. The results always came on a Saturday. I presume the thinking behind that was to give you sufficient time to compose yourself after receiving your result.

Anyway, the Thatcher household sat patiently waiting for the brown envelope to drop through the door. There had been lots of speculation as to how the contents of the envelope could be ascertained before it was opened. If it was a fat envelope that was a sign you had done well, as it contained forms to fill out for your future school. A slim envelope foretold disaster. The brown envelope which dropped through our door didn't look particularly over-nourished to me but as my mother carefully opened it and read the contents, I could see the look of relief spread across her face. I was destined for grammar school, for Foyle College no less. I was delighted. I'm not sure why but, in the background, there had always been this understanding that getting into the grammar system was much better than being excluded from it. Subsequent to my success I was feted in an appropriately modest way throughout the family and was delighted to find the odd half crown or florin being slipped into my welcoming hand. But this was just the start of the process – there was more to this new school malarkey than met the eye. There was uniform to consider, sportswear to buy, all in all a sudden burden on the family finances which I am not sure they had fully considered.

Regardless of cost, a good deal of the summer was spent getting kitted out for the new term. Visits were made to the appropriate suppliers of uniform, Brownlow's on Carlisle Road as far as I remember, for the crimson blazer, bought slightly too large to allow for growth and to avoid requiring replacement too quickly. Looking back, the simple act of moving school must have cost a fortune, a fact which may have encouraged families to select a school with less expensive uniform requirements. Towards the end of August we had invested in an array of new clothing for school: a blazer, a couple of pairs of new trousers, (short, naturally, all boys aged eleven were still wearing shorts at that time) a grey pullover with the appropriate school markings, school socks, P.E kit, new plimsolls, football boots, and of course new shoes. I was blissfully unaware of the money that was being invested in my future and the scrimping and saving it must have taken to kit me out in all this regalia, and I'm sure I was entirely ungrateful.

As all this change came along, daily life continued more or less as normal. I was still an active member of the cub scouts and continued to sing in the choir. The Cubs met weekly, we were a pack of about thirty led by our intrepid Akela, with whom I immediately fell in love. Her role was to guide us through a maze of activities. We were all particularly keen to work towards badges which could be gained for proficiency in myriad areas: knot tying, cooking, woodcraft, and my special favourite, the artist's badge.

I will never forget it. Three of us were cloistered in a side room and given our task: draw a farmyard scene. Having spent lots of time on my uncle's farm, I felt really confident of my ability to produce a lifelike reproduction of a typical farmyard. All three of us painted industriously for about half an hour before we were told to stop and bring our efforts in for adjudication. I handed my work over, feeling that I had done justice to the task. We studied our judges' faces anxiously as we waited for their comments. I was more than a little puzzled as they seemed to spend more time over my effort than the others. Finally, it was announced that we had all passed but I was singled out for a special mention. I had to contain my sense of pride as my work was displayed to my fellow Cubs but was disconcerted to see the grins spread across their faces. It finally dawned on me that my chickens had all been drawn with four legs! Latterly I thought the idea ought to have been pitched to the owners of the Kentucky Fried conglomerate as a means of doubling their profits. Despite my fellow Cubs' mirth I had my badge to wear proudly on my sleeve. I may say more of my artistic skills anon.

A NEW LAND

In August 1960 my father decided it was time to visit his brothers and sister, whom he had not seen for some time. His brother, Uncle Ken after whom I was named, used to visit us from time to time with his wife, Aunt Ede, and his brother-in-law, Uncle Archie, regularly sent us two jars of honey from his hives in Yorkshire. Uncle Ken regularly sent a postal order for ten shillings for my birthday and at Christmas. Archie was married to my Aunt Cath, by all accounts my father's favourite. They lived on an estate near Malton in North Yorkshire, where Uncle Archie was the gardener for the big house.

This would be my second visit to England. I had previously gone to stay with my Uncle Eric, Aunt Eileen, and their family in York. I have no memory of how or why this trip came about, perhaps it was a cheap holiday for me or maybe my mother needed a bit of a rest. Anyway, I found myself en route for York on the Heysham boat in the company of Aunt Eileen's brother Jim, who had been selected to accompany me on the trip. The single memory of my journey with Jim was when he carefully explained to me that whenever I spoke to any one in England, they would fail to understand what I was saying. This was my first indication that there was some kind of difference between people who lived in Ireland and those who lived in England.

It was an interesting trip as my uncle was a soldier in the British Army and living in a barracks in York. Every morning I would be awakened by the sound of military activity: bugle calls, men marching purposely hither and thither, all the trappings of military life. Aunt Eileen showed me around York with its city walls and we went to visit the Railway Museum, which I found fascinating. It was a short trip but I was pleased to find that in fact I had little difficulty in communicating with the natives.

As I was saying, Father had decided it was time to show his handsome son to his sister and as many of his brothers as we could possibly visit. We set off from Waterside Station, where else, and for the second time I found myself on the overnight sailing to Heysham. We had no accommodation booked as my father knew how the world worked. Once on board he slipped a few shillings to the purser and hey presto, we were nicely set up in a fairly comfortable cabin. When I asked about this, I was informed that there were a lot of ex-Royal Navy sailors working the ferries and they were more than happy to help former colleagues. On disembarking we boarded a train for Bristol. I definitely recall that this trip included using the rail tunnel under the Severn Estuary, the longest railway tunnel in England at four miles in length.

Eventually we reached Bristol where we were met by Uncle Harry, who took us by car to his home in Radstock in Somerset. Radstock was situated a few miles from the village of Camerton, which my father had left as a boy to join the navy. Uncle Harry lived in quite a large house on the edge of the village with his wife, Aunt Dinah. Naturally, we were made very welcome. Uncle Harry was an agent for an insurance company and his house was rather beautiful, not unlike the house that William, Richmal Crompton's loveable little boy, might have lived in, all redbrick and surrounded by lawn. He kept rabbits and had a small kitchen garden at the side of the house, supplemented by an allotment within a few yards of their kitchen. As I was to find out, Aunt Dinah loved to cook.

Since it was my father's intention to introduce me to as many of my relatives as possible, we had a fairly hectic round of visits to assorted cousins and more elderly uncles and aunts who remembered Fred, as they called my father, as a little boy. One of them, a great aunt who still lived alone in the cottage in which she had been born, had become totally blind. As she ran her fingers over my face, she declared that I was a Thatcher through and through. We visited Camerton, the place of my father's birth, saw the cottage where he had grown up, walked through the fields he would have crossed to get to school, and took the path to the church he had attended to sit in the pew where he had sat. He pointed out the more luxurious pew used by the local squire, with its built-in fireplace to add comfort on cold winter Sundays. We stopped at the village pub to see if there was anyone there whom he might remember from his youth. He was a little disappointed that there wasn't. Perhaps to compensate, my father, the teetotaller, consented to Uncle Harry buying me a half pint of local cider. After all, we were in Somerset.

We packed a lot into the week we spent with Uncle Harry. We toured the countryside, visiting Stonehenge before it became a protected monument. We went to Avebury to see the stone circle and spent a day in Salisbury to visit the cathedral. Glastonbury and its Tor and legends of King Arthur were also fitted in, and of course we had to go and see the Cheddar Gorge with its cave. We also went underground at the less well-known Wookey Hole and heard tales of its mysterious witch. Wells with its beautiful cathedral was also on our list of sights to be visited. Needless to say, all these places were still unaffected by the mass tourism they attract nowadays. It's hard to believe just how much there was to see and do in a week in Somerset. The memories remain fresh in my mind to this day.

As I previously stated, Aunt Dinah loved to cook and Uncle Harry loved to grow things for her to cook. There were meals set before us that I recall to this day, nothing particularly grand, just delicious. On the first day, we sat down to a beautiful dinner of pie and vegetables freshly dug from the garden just a few yards from the table. I remember helping dig the potatoes that morning and being somewhat dismissive of Uncle Harry's insistence on gathering up even the tiniest of the crop. When I tasted them I understood why: rarely have I tasted potatoes so sweet and tender since. Later, when I wondered what was in the pie which had been the centrepiece of the meal, I was informed that it was rabbit. Then I understood that Uncle Harry's rabbit hutches contained food rather than floppy-eared sentimental pets with dark, doe-like eyes. I think as a special treat for my father, who must at some stage have expressed some enthusiasm for it, Aunt Dinah went to the butcher to buy an ox heart, which she produced as the piece de resistance for our final dinner. I was never a reluctant eater and consumed my portion with the ultimate good grace and elegance. The other delicacy we had was a carry-out from the local chip shop: faggot and chips, otherwise known as pig's trotters. My only complaint was that it required a lot of hard work to get the meat out of the trotters, but when you did it was definitely worth the effort.

All too soon our time in Somerset was over and once again we were on the train. This time our destination was Castleford to visit Uncle Ken and Ant Ede. I knew nothing about Castleford – it was a northern town was about the extent of my knowledge – but I knew a little more about this uncle and aunt. They had been to visit us when we lived in Bond's Hill and were also the senders of gifts for both Christmas and birthdays. The time spent with them was brief, a couple of days at most, during which my Uncle Charlie came for an afternoon. It was the only time I met him; he lived somewhere in South Wales, both he and Ken were former coal miners who had been forced to move by the closure of pits in Somerset. My single memory of this part of our trip was a visit to a glass factory in neighbouring Doncaster, if I looked hard enough, I might still be able to locate the miniature bottle I was given as a souvenir.

We were nearing the end of our trip and were heading for Malton in North Yorkshire, where we were to stay with Uncle Archie and Aunt Cath. Aunt Cath was my father's favourite sibling and it was because of her mistreatment by their stepmother that he had argued with his father and eventually left home. Arch was the head gardener in a small estate and their house was part of the farmyard there. Arch took great pride in his work and I recall being fascinated with the fruit and flowers he produced, mostly for use in the big house. As he proudly showed my father round his greenhouses I saw figs for the first time, peaches ripening against the wall, beautiful pears and quince and of course his beehives, which produced the honey he sent us every year without fail.

Throughout our stay the weather had been glorious and during our sojourn with Uncle Archie and Aunt Cath, I was allowed to play outside in the garden. The previous evening I had noticed a boy and girl of a similar age to myself playing on a swing suspended from a large tree a few hundred yards away. I decided to investigate and made my way round to the big tree, which was situated in the lawn stretched out before a rather handsome house. Seeing no sign of the children I made my way up to the front door of the house and rang the bell. A few seconds later the door opened and I was met by a young girl dressed in black with a frilly apron and bonnet. She looked at me in horror and demanded to know what on earth I was doing ringing the bell at the front door. I politely inquired if the little boy whom I had seen the night before would like to come out to play. I was given a lecture on my station in life, told that I had no business calling at the front door and if indeed I had any business doing anything I was to call at the back door as the front door was reserved for proper people. Given the commotion, it was not long before the lady of the house appeared and, after establishing my identity, very gently explained that the children were at their lessons but if I were to call back in the afternoon they might well come out to play.

And out to play they did come, accompanied by a maid. All I recall is taking turns on the swing, with very little by way of conversation. They probably didn't understand a word I said. I believe this was my first encounter with the notion of them and us; then as now I remain particularly unaffected by it. All too quickly our trip to England was over and we were soon back home getting ready for the Big School.

MEANWHILE BACK AT THE CHALK FACE

Luckily, I was not the only person from the area to be going to Foyle. I think there were at least three of us facing the daunting walk to Lawrence Hill and the imposing three-storey building overlooking Strand Road and the River Foyle beyond. As the expectation grew apace, so did the rumours concerning what lay before first-years. There were stories of various induction rituals, the least of which involved being thrown over the wall which bordered the playground. Unlike today's new entrants there was no such thing as an induction day, you simply turned up and were grateful.

And turn up we did, like lambs to the slaughter all neatly trussed up in our new uniforms and shiny black shoes. We gathered together in the assembly hall to be placed in our form. I was in 1B which I think signified average; 1C contained all those who had the lowest qualifying scores in the test, plus those who had failed the Eleven-plus but whose parents were fortunate enough to have sufficient financial backing to be able to afford the fees. The morning was spent with our form teacher, who explained how the school worked and what we were to study. The day was divided into nine periods and in total we would study approximately fourteen different subjects. The day began at 9:00 am and had pauses for assembly, break, and lunch. The school had no canteen, so pupils had to cater for themselves by bringing a packed lunch or going home. It was also possible to go into town to one of the numerous cafes along the Strand Road. I was fortunate as I could go home for lunch; we lived less than ten minutes from school and five minutes to get back as it was downhill on the return journey. On day one we finished at noon, so armed with our timetable for the coming year, we were sent home.

It should have been no surprise that we were soon to be fleeced just as the little lambs we were. On the afternoon of the first day we were expected to buy whatever textbooks we would require for the year. Back to Lawrence Hill we went, armed with whatever few pounds we could persuade our parents to give us. It was open season for those who had been equally fleeced the year before and I suppose it was for many a subtle introduction to capitalism. Our aim was to acquire all the necessary books as quickly as possible; the second years' ambition was to get as much as possible from the most gullible first years. The trick was to ensure that you only bought the books you actually needed, in the best condition, as you knew that you would be reselling them in a year's time. When negotiations were concluded it only remained to go home and explain to parents where all their cash had gone.

Next day, education began in earnest. From having sat comfortably in one room from the start of the school day until the final bell, you had to get used to moving from one subject to another and from one room to another. My nightmare was remembering to bring the correct textbooks on the right day – woe betide you if you turned up for a history class clutching a maths textbook. It was also important to get to know the idiosyncrasies of individual teachers. There were those whose reputation preceded them; take Mr Craig for example, inexplicably nicknamed 'Mo', who considered himself a cut above most of those set before him. Or Mr Leclerc, known as 'Clapp', who taught us geography and struggled with discipline. Then there were others like Mr Connolly, the Headmaster, and Mr Gillanders, his deputy, who both ruled with a rod of iron. For some reason I have no clear recollection of who taught me what during that first year of secondary education but I soon settled into the rhythm of school life. You quickly got the hang of rushing from one end of the school to the other, staying on the right side of corridors, and using the correct staircase to ascend and descend. As I said, the bit I found most difficult was having the right books for the right subject. Getting it wrong usually meant some kind of punishment and I became quite adept at writing lines.

Foyle divided its students into 'Houses', based I presume on the system operated in English public schools. I suppose it added something to the kudos of the school, setting it apart from the intermediate schools which were the destination of those unsuccessful in the Eleven-plus. Foyle had four 'Houses': Andrews, Lawrence, Montgomery, and Springham, the first three named after distinguished 'old boys' and Springham after the school's founder. On closer inspection, I wonder just how distinguished those 'old boys' were in the light of modern thinking. I was put in Lawrence due to my family connection, my cousin having been a member some years previously. It was said that housemasters ran their eyes over new admissions in order to get the best pupils for their house. If it was the school's intention to create a sense of loyalty, camaraderie, and identity, the house system was very successful. The annual competition for the House Cup engendered much passion at every level and being a member of the winning house at the end of the year would add an inch or two to your bearing.

Secondary school put much more emphasis on sport than we had been used to at The Model. We were actually timetabled for P.E, whereas in primary school it seemed to be entirely at the whim of the teacher. We had P.E twice a week and an afternoon dedicated to games. P.E took place in what was laughingly called 'the gym', essentially a large space which might once have been used as the chapel in days long gone. We had to change at the back; the changing room was a row of pegs on which to hang your clothes. With no privacy and no showers, you just allowed any sweat you might have worked up to dry quietly throughout the day. If you forgot your kit, you simply did it in your undergarments and bare feet. P.E mostly consisted of 'physical jerks', an endless round of press-ups, star jumps, running on the spot, and so forth. P.E teachers of the time seemed mostly ex-army types, so I suppose we were grateful not to be constantly running obstacle courses.

Games afternoons took place at the school's sports pitches at

Springtown, located about a mile from the school on what was then the boundary of the city. It was at Springtown that we were introduced to rugby. Most of us were footballers of one sort or the other; I was more 'the other' and when matches were organised at street level I never expected to be anybody's first pick. No matter, skill at football didn't necessarily equate with skill at rugby. We were all inducted with a modicum of success into the art of the game. Everyone was expected to take part, from the least to the most skilled, from the most physically adept to the seven-stone weaklings, we all had to get stuck in. Games afternoons were never cancelled, no matter what the weather threw at us some kind of sporting activity took place. Even worse, the art of becoming a rugby player seemed to instil some kind of madness into us – we never felt we had had a good game unless our kit was plastered in mud. Few houses would have had the luxury of a washing machine in those days, so it fell to our patient mothers to add P.E and rugby kit to their weekly chores.

As for personal hygiene, that too took a very back seat. The changing rooms, as they were laughingly referred to at Springtown, would have pleased the Spartans. Facilities consisted of a tin hut about twenty foot long and ten foot broad, into which approximately sixty youths were distilled to change in and out of their clothes. Showers it would seem were yet to be invented or not essential for young boys, because there were none to be had either at Springtown or in school. In my case that didn't really matter – I was no more than ten minutes from home – but there were numerous boys facing a journey of up to an hour with mud caking slowly on their face and hands.

Annually, the school organised a cross-country run. Most boys dreaded it. The course was I suppose no more than three miles long, wending its way through the countryside which surrounded the playing fields at Springtown, taking in stretches of the old Lough Swilly railway track and the sandpits at the bottom of Duncreggan Road, and finishing back at Springtown. The first time, I completed the course and finished a respectable number of places from the end. The second year, I finished in the top twenty, much to the astonishment of my friends and teachers. It was to my good fortune that no one had noticed I had jumped onto the rear of a coal lorry, which had facilitated my pace over a good half mile of the course. This was the first and last time I ever remember being dishonest in a sporting context. I have no idea what possessed me to do it; I even recall that as I approached the finishing line, I held back to give my time a more believable appearance. For a brief moment, I was even concerned I might end up being selected for the school cross-country team. Luckily, that didn't happen.

PRANKS AND PUNISHMENT

There were two highlights to the week. On Mondays, immediately after lunch, we went swimming. Swimming had been a staple at Foyle. The former Londonderry Academical Institution building on Academy Road, where boarders were once housed, had a swimming pool of sorts where my cousin said he learned the art of swimming. It was by our time in a state of dereliction, so we were sent to the newly built Municipal Baths in William Street.

I remember quite clearly that we had to be back in school by 2:35 pm for Latin. We seldom made it in time, I can't think why. On Thursday morning we had Art. This class took place in 'The Tech' at the bottom of Lawrence Hill and our teacher was Miss Mulhern, later to be my colleague, Mary Hughes. She was the most patient of teachers. Ever since my drawing of the chicken with four legs I had more or less abandoned any hope of success with art, but Mary persisted. She knew my mother did all my homework: 'Tell your mother she did well today', she would say regularly, as my mark for homework soared to the dizzy heights of four and a half out of ten. I remain as ungifted today as I was then.

Of my other teachers, with one or two exceptions, I recall little. I believe my first encounter with French was under the guidance of Mr. Curzon Mowbray, a man small in stature but immense in presence. He was a gifted linguist and an ardent fan of cricket, who looked after the First XI cricket team for decades. We may have had Mr Craig (aka 'Mo') for English, which often meant interminable lessons spent parsing extremely contrived sentences and very little else. Later in my academic career I would have Mo for History, the subject for which he had a real passion.

Mo taught in Room 4 which was adjacent to the main 'Boys' entrance. His room was the embodiment of the old-fashioned classroom. There were about twenty single desks and right at the back four desks probably left over from the nineteenth century, which could accommodate about eight reasonably sized small boys. On one occasion Mo had become rather fraught at the lack of homework he was collecting and completely lost the run of himself. Striding down from his dais he launched himself in my direction – by good fortune I was not his target but the boy immediately behind me was. He grabbed the poor fellow by the hair and dragged him across two of these antiquated desks in order to berate him in front of us all. He was then sent to stand outside the door. The remainder of the lesson was conducted in absolute silence.

Next day we had Mo again. The object of Mo's wrath appeared before him with his head swathed in a crepe bandage. He had just put it on in the toilets immediately before the lesson. No words were exchanged but the lesson was conducted in an exemplary manner by Mo. There was no hint of contrition on his part but we understood it would be best if any provocation was avoided. We had a good laugh about it afterwards but he knew and we knew that there were boundaries which ought not to be crossed.

Mo was a fervent believer in the might of the British Empire, he also believed himself to be a cut above the rest of us. I recall him once describing one of the more wealthy families in the city as having made their money in 'trade', the ultimate of all put-downs. I was also in the lesson in which he became slightly overwrought and decided that one of my classmates, whose parents had arrived in Derry from India about fifty years previously, was personally responsible for the Indian Mutiny and the atrocities inflicted on the British at the time. The unfortunate object of his anger was made to stand on top of his desk beneath a naked lightbulb with flies buzzing around it until the bell sounded and we moved to our next class.

Mo idolised Winston Churchill; he had a Collie dog that he named Bracken after one of Churchill's advisors. He was mad about The Duke of Marlborough, one of the great man's illustrious ancestors, and taught the topic for A-level. He had a portrait of Winston which hung directly behind his desk in Room 4. One morning we arrived for History to find the portrait turned to face the wall. At first we imagined there must have been a bit of an affray in a previous lesson, but soon we discovered that recently released wartime cabinet papers had disclosed that Winston had been negotiating with De Valera, with a view to the reunification of Ireland in return for the use of Irish ports during the war. Winston continued to face the wall until the school migrated to Springtown, at which point he disappeared, never to be seen again.

The last of Mo's quirks I recall was the terrible difficulties he had with names. At one stage it became so bad that we decided to keep a record of the number of different versions of one person's name he would use in the course of a lesson. To the best of my recollection I was the outright winner. In the hour and ten minutes which a double period lasted, I was addressed by twenty-three different names: 'Thrifter', 'Thrower', 'Thresher', 'Trotter', 'Trainor', and so on. How can I recall all that and yet remember so little of the content of the lessons?

Room 3 was latterly the domain of Mr Cecil Bryans, another of my History teachers who also dabbled in French and English. It was his lot to teach me French at O-level. His classes were frequently interesting but not always for the right reasons. Boys quickly learned that he was not overly difficult to wind up. His response to whatever taunt had been inflicted on him was to visit some minor violence upon his tormentor and then lead him off by the ear to visit the headmaster. The headmaster's office lay at the other end of the building and invariably, about halfway along the corridor, 'Gus' for so he was nicknamed) ended up apologising to the pupil and bringing him sheepishly back to class.

Room 3 was ideally situated for other pranks. Foyle had a little-used basement which ran the length of the building. Sometimes, students would make their way through the basement to a room directly below

Gus's, and with an abandoned plank would begin to hammer on the ceiling above them. As you might imagine, this sudden outburst of hammering would scare the life out of the occupants of the room overhead and the class would rapidly descend into chaos. Gus's room could equally fall victim to a prank from higher up. Some of the older boys would stuff an old uniform full of crumpled newspaper and at a given moment would launch it from Room 14, directly above. Poor old Gus would suddenly catch a glimpse of this 'body' falling past his window and needless to say, pandemonium would ensue.

The most elaborate prank to which I was a witness took place during a class consisting of lower-sixth scientists whose English was deemed to be weak. Poor Gus must have some free time and he was volunteered to take these so-called illiterate scientists for 'Use of English'. The class was timetabled for fifth period, just after break. We all assembled as usual and began the work we had been set. Everyone was working industriously, which was in itself slightly unusual. About ten minutes into the lesson there was a very slight explosion and suddenly the teacher's desk was engulfed in clouds of purple smoke. You can imagine the rest: teacher was trying to waft the smoke away with his gown and of course we were shouting and roaring at the top of our voices.

It transpired that two of the A-level Chemistry students, aggrieved at being forced to study English, had created a concoction of harmless chemicals which would react with whatever catalyst they had rigged up, thus setting off the explosion. No one was hurt, no damage was caused, and the incident was never mentioned again. I can still see the poor fellow gesticulating wildly with his gown, whether to disperse the fumes or usher us to safety, who can say. One of the other tricks we inflicted on poor old Mr Bryans had its genesis in the library. The library took a multiplicity of magazines, many of which contained advertisements which invited you to send a name and address to receive free examples of their wares. Since these were 'postage paid', we took great pleasure in sending off requests by the bagful, giving Cecil's name and address as the recipient. I dread to think of the amount of post which must have poured through his letterbox in the course of the year. The postman must have been relieved when the school holidays began.

Music lessons for junior classes were under the direction of Miss Rankin, a lady of a certain age who always seemed to have one stocking which was never securely attached to its suspension system. We spent a year in the assembly hall, where the piano was located, singing 'The Minstrel Boy', frequently under the stern gaze of Mr Connolly, who was there to ensure that some kind of harmony reigned. In later life I would often feel sorry for musicians who found a career in teaching; for every pupil with a genuine interest and talent there must have been hundreds who had neither ability nor interest.

Science has left only a vague imprint on my mind. Mrs Connolly, the headmaster's wife, brightened up Chemistry by creating explosions and plumes of acrid smoke from various compounds. I can still see Norman Gillespie's withering look during a Physics lesson when I asked him if I should heat the water in the test tube to more than one hundred degrees Celsius. Subsequently, I have learnt that my query wasn't as stupid as he implied. Ian McCracken came to teach us Biology, of all things. His 'lab' was on the top floor. He wasn't much older than ourselves and we thought he was 'good craic'. Thus began my fairly lengthy association with Foyle College and as such my recollections of that time are nothing but positive, though no doubt made rosy by the passage of time.

What of the building itself? It was designed and constructed in the early eighteen-hundreds and although it was built to accommodate boarders it would never have been considered fit to house the four-hundred-plus boys who were there in the 1960s. Externally it looked magnificent: in the sixties the whole front was covered in ivy, lending it an air of distinction. Internally, it left a lot to be desired. The school revolved around a central stairwell which was the principal thoroughfare for movement between classes. Imagine around four hundred boys all on the move simultaneously. Rigid rules were strictly enforced to lessen any chance of an accident. Up the front stairs, down the back stairs was the mantra by which we moved in relative harmony. It was at the foot of the main stairs in a stairwell which rose to the top of the building that the entire school seemed to congregate at break time. It was here that the free milk with which the government provided us was left out just before the bell sounded for break. Most of the four hundred plus pupils engaged in a daily melee to secure their ration of milk. 'Sarge' also ran a tuck shop from a cupboard on the corridor just outside Room 4, where we bought our crisps, Wagon Wheels, or whatever other delicacy we could afford. This was immensely popular and led to many an affray over queue jumping. I often wonder just how Sarge served so many customers in the ten minutes allocated for break. No doubt there were moments when all was not as agreeable as I remember but they have not found a permanent place in my memory.

MORE ABOUT PETS

At some time after the demise of Tinkle, our mongrel dog, my father decided that we should have another pet. One morning he arrived home with a remarkably handsome pure-black Cocker Spaniel named Flash. Being a pedigree animal, he had another much grander name on his Kennel Club papers. He settled in quite rapidly but he was hard work, he was full of energy and needed walking twice a day. A leisurely stroll around the block didn't cut the mustard; he needed serious walking to try and dissipate his zest for life and I found myself walking for miles to try and wear him out. Ultimately it was me who was worn out, Flash seemed to go on forever.

He was very affectionate with people he knew but became excessively protective of our house. In those days there were lots of callers, ranging from bread men to laundry men, bin men and brock collectors, all of whom prompted Flash to bouts of furious barking and scurrying around the house. We tolerated this behaviour for as long as possible but after the laundry man declared he would no longer come, Flash's days were numbered. Fortunately, my father found someone to take him on and we said a tearful goodbye.

Despite my mother's protests, it didn't take long before another pet made an entrance at Nicholson Terrace. Daisy the cat was a free spirit and more or less minded herself. I remember her for two things. First of all, she had kittens on my lap as I was sitting watching television. A bit of a shock, I can tell you. The second remarkable thing she did was a bit Lazarine. She disappeared for about six weeks and we had given up on ever seeing her again, when suddenly she reappeared on the coal shed roof. She had been in a serious fight and her head was partially severed from her body. My father took her to the vet, who sewed her back together, and she made an extraordinary recovery and lived happily with us for many more years. She had a great relationship with my father. She would sense when he was coming home and install herself on the garage roof to wait for him. When he arrived, she would jump down onto his shoulder and wrap herself around his neck until he reached the kitchen.

KEN THE COUNTRY BOY

While all this was happening, I was leading a kind of parallel life as a country boy. As I have explained, my mother's older sister, Aunt Mamie, had married George Foster of Creevagh, a farmer. George and Mamie had three sons, who were regarded by the family as my three older brothers. It was not unusual for me to spend an occasional night at Creevagh and indeed in the summer an occasional night might stretch into four or five weeks, which suited me just fine. For some reason which I could never fathom, George, my uncle, could never bring himself to refer to me as his nephew. I was 'the wife's sister's wee boy' and once I had worked out what it meant, I think I was quite pleased with it.

As I got a little older I was expected to participate in the day-to-day running of the farm, which for the most part I found rather pleasing. Creevagh was a mixed farm growing cereals, hay, and potatoes, alongside a small herd of milking cows, some sheep and sometimes pigs, and of course a scattering of hens and ducks without which no small farm would have been complete. Uncle George also had a milk round in the city. In the early days milk was delivered daily from a horse and cart, later to be replaced by a lorry. Prince, the horse who drew the milk cart, lived at Creevagh. Harry, the milkman, walked the couple of miles from the city every morning, rain, hail, or shine, to harness him before they set off on their round. Prince was a magnificent animal, resplendent in his harness which jingled as he trotted along the road.

Life on the farm began rather early. The first stirrings could be heard from around 5:30 am when, in summer, the cows had to be brought in for milking. This wasn't so bad in the summer but in early spring or late autumn, when it could be quite chilly and damp, it was more of a struggle. When I was staying I would usually get up at this time to help; I suppose I was ten or eleven and considered sufficiently sensible to know my way around cows. In the very early days the cows were milked by hand. I was completely useless at hand milking and would have been more of a hindrance than a help, but I was sufficiently competent to carry buckets of fresh milk from the byre to the spotlessly clean dairy, where the frothing milk was transferred into ten-gallon churns to await collection that morning by the tanker from the Leckpatrick Dairy.

When the milking was finished it was time for breakfast, usually a hearty fry with bacon, eggs, and sausages. There was little talk of cholesterol in those days – you mopped up the residual grease with a slice of bread. The driver of the milk tanker strangely always seemed to arrive just as the pan went onto the range. He brought news from all arts and parts as well as from neighbouring farms, making him a very welcome guest.

With breakfast consumed, the main work of the day began. Living and working on a farm, everything depended on the weather and the season. Quite often I would have been there in spring, which was the time to prepare the fields and sow the crops. Uncle George would frequently rent land from neighbouring farmers and depending on its quality he would plant potatoes, or perhaps hay or barley. In those days it was economically possible to employ at least one permanent farmhand, taking on more when the work required it. Immediately after breakfast the trailer would be hitched up and off we went to whatever task was to be done. Usually we were there within fifteen to twenty minutes, but when I think back, that ride on the trailer was at the same time exciting and scary. Nowadays it would be utterly out of the question to have ten-year-olds standing trying to balance on the back of a speeding trailer, but it was terrific and no one ever came to any harm. Weather permitting, we would be in the field all day. To keep us fed, someone would turn up at about 10:30 am with tea, served in milk bottles, and thick slices of homemade scone bread plastered in butter and jam. This would be repeated at noon and 3:00 pm. At the later tea, one person would have to go home to attend to the milking. Scone bread has never tasted the way it did sitting out in the fields, washing it down with the lukewarm tea from those pint milk bottles and listening to the men telling tall tales or discussing the ways of the world.

Uncle George was a firm believer in tradition and potatoes formed a major part of his cash crop. Preparations would begin early in the year and fields were ploughed and harrowed for planting. Around the beginning of April the sowing began. In those days the seeds were dropped by hand by two people sitting on top of a machine, which formed the drill as it was drawn slowly over the ground by the ubiquitous wee grey Massey Ferguson. There followed a period of care when furrows would be moulded up and once the tops began to appear a careful watch was kept for the dreaded blight. In order to maintain the crop they would be chemically treated with a sprayer, which at the time seemed perfectly sensible.

The real excitement of the potato season came in early autumn when it was time to gather them in. This required a considerable workforce which was assembled quite quickly and simply. The tractor and trailer were driven down to Central Drive in Creggan and from nowhere a dozen or so youths appeared, climbed onto the trailer and set off to the field. Gathering potatoes was backbreaking, interminable work which went on for days, often when the weather had taken a turn for the worse. Potatoes were spun out of the ground by the digger mounted on the back of the tractor and pairs of gatherers scooped them into baskets, then filled them into bags which were transferred back to the farm for sorting. Their final destination was Cyprus, to be used as seed for next year's early crop.

On reaching the farm the bags' contents were sorted into seed and ware potatoes. The seed potatoes were put into sacks which were sealed and stored in the barn, to await the arrival of the inspector who would decide if they were fit for export. Ware potatoes were for local consumption. I can only recall one occasion when they were turned down and had to be looked at again before being submitted for a second inspection. The gatherers were paid at the end of each day, probably working on the principle that some might fall by the wayside having had their will broken by the tough nature of the work. My self-esteem took a bit of a blow when I noticed that whilst my fellow workers were getting maybe ten or fifteen shillings for their day's labour, I was lucky to get half a crown. I was sufficiently wise to close my fist tightly round it and keep my counsel. After all, good old Uncle George was keeping me in cheap cigarettes, to which I was rapidly becoming addicted.

From time to time there would be jobs which required travel, sometimes to exotic locations such as Limavady or Carndonagh but more frequently to the cattle market on Lecky Road. On one occasion I remember setting off to Limavady in the car with Uncle George to look at some pigs. The animals were the property of a local publican who ran a piggery at the back of the pub. After some haggling, which took place naturally enough in the public bar, the deal was struck and off set Uncle George on some other mission, leaving me, aged eleven, to await someone who would collect me and the pig and bring us back to Creevagh. All well and good, you may think. The pig however had other plans and began to give birth to a litter, much to my consternation. So, after a suitable time to allow the pig to recover, I set off for home, not with one animal but with a sow and about ten piglets. The poor old sow was afforded very little sympathy or postnatal care before being driven off to her new abode.

On another of my rural adventures, Uncle George had purchased some sheep and they had to be brought home. No problem, you might think, but no lorries were available to transport them. So, it was decided that they were to be walked the fifteen or so miles to Sheriff's Mountain. Can you imagine walking about fifty sheep along the main road to Derry? I was only required for the last few miles, essentially the bit that took them through the town. Every garden gate had to be 'kept' to prevent sheep eating flowers and lawns. You can imagine the amount of shepherding required to move them from The Garden City down Culmore Road, along The Strand, up Duncreggan Road and finally up Glen Road, until we reached the country again at Shaw's Lane. We got them safely installed in their new home but even the couple of miles I did left me very stiff and sore the next morning. This wasn't quite as strange an activity as it might seem as at that time people in Derry were fairly used to animals being driven through the streets, either to market or to the 'Scotch Boat' moored behind The Guildhall for further transportation.

One day it was announced that we were having an outing to Carndonagh. There was no clearly defined purpose, I think things on the farm were up to date and an excursion was called for. It was a Fair Day in Carn and there were lots of stalls hawking all sorts of goods. I bought a rather large penknife from one of the stallholders, who was marketing it as the same style of knife used in the assassination of Prime Minister Patrice Lamumbo in the Congo. Why on earth that resonated with me, I have no idea. The knife fell to pieces a few days later; it was obviously a single-use weapon of political assassination. The rest of the day in Carn was spent sitting in the car outside a pub, being refreshed from time to time with minerals and crisps sent from within.

One less savoury memory which has never left me relates to a late summer afternoon when we were in a field just behind Creggan in the area which would later become known as Piggery Ridge. I think we had been working at hay. In the adjacent field there was suddenly a group of boys and girls who had come out from the neighbouring Termonbacca House, presumably to play. Almost at once they were pursued by a group of nuns who were shouting instructions at the children and telling them to get back to wherever it was they had come from. I could hear the swish of the canes with which the nuns were equipped. When I asked what this was all about I was told these were 'orphans' who were taken into care by the church. It was a long time before I was to understand the truth of it. At the time, I thanked my lucky stars it wasn't me being driven in like an animal from the fields.

On occasion, I also got to accompany Uncle George to the market held mid-week at Rossville Street, where farmers from all around the country gathered to buy and sell their animals. Many deals were done unofficially and I can recall some where a couple of donkeys could be bought for a pound. For me this was all terrific entertainment, whilst at the same time expanding my understanding of how the world worked. People from all kinds of farms, large and small, gathered to wheel and deal and when business was done to repair the local pubs, of which there were many, for refreshment. Quite frequently refreshments became excessive and it was not unusual to see men being led rather reluctantly to their transport home. The market was also populated with a variety of characters who made their living from setting up deals or as 'cow wallopers', whose job, as the name implies, was to herd the animals to and from different locations, sometimes near at hand and sometimes through the streets for transportation on the Glasgow boat.

Whilst Uncle George refreshed himself I was forced to amuse myself. There wasn't much for a wee boy to do but hang around the entrance to the bar and wait for the 'refreshing' to end. Still, there was one shop I always liked to visit, McLaughlin's hardware store on William Street. I just loved their stock; they had, so it seemed, everything. The most I could ever stretch to was a pair of 'whangs'. To the uninitiated, a 'whang' is a thin strip of leather, mostly used as a bootlace but, at the appropriate time, also served to hang a chestnut on. You could buy two for a penny. I also enjoyed mooching around the various parts of the market, where you were never quite sure what to expect. One day I watched as a farmer opened the boot of his car to show four fairly newborn calves lying on a bed of straw. As best as I could make out, he sold them all for a couple of pounds. Another day, Uncle decided that I could do with a horse and after a bit of trading, a horse, or rather a pony, was bought sight unseen. The pony was brought from a field near Saint Johnston a few days later. Uncle George employed Jim Harkin, one of the regular cattle dealers and master of all trades, to ride him from Saint Johnston to Creevagh. Allegedly Tom was my pony; I taught myself to ride him and had great fun with him. Eventually Uncle got a good offer and as I watched Tom disappear down the road in a horsebox, it transpired that he wasn't mine at all.

There were harder days too. It wasn't easy standing in an open field walling potatoes taken from a pit where they had been stored all winter. The frost and icy wind would quickly turn your fingers blue. I also remember sitting all day in a darkened shed cutting potatoes for the spring planting, only coming out blinking in the light when the job was completed. The worst of all jobs must have been thinning turnips. All day you were on your knees in the mud, crawling along an interminable drill of barely sprouting turnips, using your bare hands to pluck out some plants to make room for those which were left to grow to a commercial size. When you finally reached the end of a drill and hoped for some satisfaction in a job well done, you turned about and began the backbreaking task of returning along the adjacent drill. Equally boring but far less painful was planting potatoes. In the highly mechanised age of the early sixties this required two people to sit on a contraption which was harnessed to the tractor, a 'potato dropper' I think it was called. As the tractor opened a drill, a bell rang and it was your job to drop a potato down a chute and into the drill. Not a very taxing task but infinitely boring. As the tractor made its way relentlessly up and down the field you hoped that something, anything, would happen to relieve the monotony of it all.

Summer on the farm was the best time of year. There was the long stretch in the evenings and days were spent out in the fields bringing in the hay, or stooking corn as it came off the binder. The binder was a magnificent contraption which seemed to have at least a million working parts, a fault in any one of which was followed by an explosion of oaths and a lot of tinkering with spanners, screwdrivers, and as a last resort a hammer, until things began to tick over smoothly once more. The binder was a wonderful invention; not only did it cut the corn but it arranged it along a belt, gathered it into bunches, knotted the sheaf with binder twine and ejected the freshly cut cereal behind it. Men then followed the binder, gathering up the sheaves and stooking them upright in groups of three to allow the wind to dry them, before they were taken away some days later to be stored in stacks in the stack garden. Eventually the thresher would arrive and a day would be spent threshing the corn, taking the grain away in ten-stone bags.

The building of the corn stack is another lost art. They were built on footings of branches and bushes to lift them slightly off the ground, to prevent damp seeping up and rotting the corn. When they were topped out they were thatched to make them waterproof. The final part of the process was to tie them down with ropes twisted out of straw, secured across the top of the stack to keep the thatch on. I became quite adept at twisting these 'sugans'. The stacks became a great breeding ground for rats and when the day came to do the threshing, men would come with their dogs to catch and dispatch as many of the fleeing rodents as possible. All of this was skilful work and very labour intensive but there was great satisfaction in a job well done. I doubt that exists today, when a man drives an enormous combine harvester into a field and leaves an hour later with the job complete and little evidence of his work, except for a number of round bales covered in black polythene.

Making hay was another weather-dependent and labour-intensive task. I was too young to have seen fields mown by a man with a scythe, but I saw men 'open' a field with one. Opening a field meant making a space to allow the tractor and reaper to enter the field to begin cutting, without wasting some of the valuable crop. Successful haymaking required a spell of good weather, ideally unbroken sunshine accompanied by a warm breeze to turn the mown grass into hay. Once the hay was mown it lay overnight in the fields in long strips, then it was 'tedded', that is turned manually by men using pitchforks, before being gathered up into 'cocks', small accumulations of hay about two feet tall which were eventually made into 'tram cocks', which were about ten feet tall. Finally, the hay was drawn either into a sheltered corner of the field or back to the farm, where it was made into stacks in the same fashion the corn was. The larger cocks were moved by a tractor using a wire rope placed around the hay. It was then sliped to the appropriate location for stacking.

It was during this process that I had my closest brush with disaster. I would ride on the back of the tractor driven by one of my cousins and my job was to run the wire rope in a loop round the tram cock and attach it to the rear of the tractor. I would then sit on top of the hay as it was dragged along. I got a bit carried away and was standing on top of the hay when I suddenly lost my balance and tipped forward towards the tractor. It was only by good fortune that I fell onto the bars on the back and managed to cling on, otherwise I would have fallen under the hay and been dragged underneath it for hundreds of yards, more than likely coming to a sorry end and causing no end of misery to my nearest and dearest. The only visible evidence of my fall was an enormous black eye, which I managed somehow to explain away. I knew that if the truth had come out it would have put an end to my days on the farm. I never ever mentioned my mishap to anybody; this is the first time for many years I have allowed myself to dwell on it and I feel relieved that I have managed thus far to live happily ever after.

Not long after that particular summer, hay making became much more mechanised when the baler replaced the building of haystacks. The era of labour-intensive haymaking came to an end but my involvement with haymaking continued. When mechanisation eventually reached the North West, Uncle invested in a baler. Since his farm wasn't nearly big enough to justify the purchase, he hired it out to the country, that is to say he took his baler to other farms and baled their hay for a price. I was hired out, very cheaply, with the baler. My job was to insert the steel rods into the compacted hay to create a bale. This meant I had to wait for the right moment to push the two rods through, follow them up with a length of baler wire, then loop the wire together to make the bale. Not an overly taxing job but you had to be quick and avoid the piston, which thudded relentlessly back and forth to compact the hay.

Working on a farm always carried a risk and as I grew older I frequently saw the negative side of rural life. When hay was replaced by silage I was once more expected to lend a hand. My role was to drive the tractor back and forth on top of the grass as it was built into the silage pit. Not a complicated task but, as the grass built up, you could find yourself driving to within a couple of feet of a fifteen-foot drop. Whether by good fortune or good driving I never experienced a moment of anxiety but tragedy was never more than a hair's breadth away. On more than one occasion I encountered people whose lives had been transformed by accidents: men who had severed a limb while working on a threshing machine or lost a family member to a tractor accident. I am glad to say that never again did I have a scrape with disaster whilst working on the farm.

THE INS AND OUTS OF COUNTRY LIFE

Living in the country, it didn't take too long to get an understanding of how life works; all you had to do was stand around and keep your eyes open. My first acquaintance with the facts of life came when cows began to get a little frisky. When I inquired as to what was going on I was told they were 'abulling', which meant that they had an inclination to visit a bull. I was still a bit mystified, being unaware of the social etiquette of bovine dating systems. Eventually I was allowed to walk with the cow to the neighbouring farm as she paid a visit to her friend the bull. I left fully apprised of the niceties of the reproductive cycle of animals.

At some time pigs began to figure in local farms as a good way to make money fairly easily. It wasn't long until a number of sows were installed in Creevagh. After a while they produced litters and the piglets were to be fattened up to produce bacon for the breakfast tables of Ulster. To facilitate the fattening process, male pigs were to be castrated. I had no idea what this meant but one afternoon a local farmer arrived to see to the pigs. I watched as he busied himself preparing to do whatever it was he was going to do. The piglets were gathered into a pen and a new razor blade was produced. I recoiled in horror as I watched the operation unfold, feeling an uneasy quiver run through my body, especially in the nether regions. The two farm dogs had an unexpected treat as the removed organs were thrown to them to gobble up. I felt then that my grasp of the facts of life were sufficiently complete and ever since I have had some sympathy for male farm animals. Whilst their ultimate destination might have been the dinner table, they had many indignities to suffer along the way.

One of the other features of farm life I found rather endearing was the competitive nature of those who worked on the land. Almost any farming activity could be made competitive, from who could plough the straightest furrow to who could eat the greatest number of potatoes at the dinner table. I witnessed otherwise sensible men be drawn into eating competitions, indeed I may have taken part in the odd one myself. It was not unusual to witness a grown man consume upwards of twenty potatoes at a sitting, just to prove he was better than the person across the table. Aching bellies and terrible outbreaks of wind were often a consequence of such overeating.

Feats of strength were another area where competition could be fierce. I still recall the pleasure I experienced when I finally succeeded in lifting a fifty-six-pound weight off the ground and my further delight when I was able to lift it above my head. Men also took great pride in their prowess at offloading sacks from a lorry or trailer. The greatest test of all was the ability to manhandle sacks of grass seed or Guano, pronounced locally 'Jew Anna. These were usually delivered in bags weighing sixteen stone, about one hundred kilos in today's money. These huge sacks were carried from a lorry and stacked in a shed by men who did their utmost not to show the slightest sign of weakness or distress. The merest hint of a slackening of pace or buckling of knee would lead to hoots of derision from their fellow workers. Strangely, these feats of strength often led to a debate as to whether a sixteen-stone bag of grass seed would be lighter than a similar-sized bag of Guano! I think this conundrum was usually put forward for my benefit.

BACK TO SCHOOL

It was customary that I be dragged back from the country about a week before the new school year, probably to knock off some of the rough edges accrued during the summer months. I must say it was quite pleasant to become a townie once again. It was certainly agreeable to wake up and know that it was time enough to get up at 8:00 am, rather than the 6:00 am start dictated by milking times. School resumed without much ado; the only difference was that I had been promoted from 1B to 2A. Presumably I had done sufficiently well in the examinations to warrant it. My parents were naturally rather pleased but I was more wary, the competition would be rather stiffer and as we all know what goes up can also come down.

The school had at last managed to recruit a properly qualified PE teacher, a Mr Roy Seddon, a Yorkshire man and a footballer of some ability. He would play for Derry City and was a member of the team which won the Cup in the mid-1960s. We were delighted with his arrival as he dragged Foyle's sports offering into the twentieth century. Soon we were playing volleyball, doing gymnastics after school, and generally broadening our sporting horizons. We also went to the swimming baths in William Street for half an hour on a Monday afternoon. Rugby however remained the predominant sport. Our games afternoon was dedicated to rugby and for those who were chosen to represent the school, Saturday was also a rugby day. I was lucky enough to be chosen and so Saturdays were spent either at Springtown or travelling the length and breadth of Ulster playing against other schools.

This wasn't so bad if you were playing local schools like Limavady but often fixtures were against Belfast schools. Travelling was interesting and necessitated meeting at the Waterside railway station for the journey to Ballymena, Belfast, or wherever it happened to be. On these away games you were fed by the opposition, sometimes rather sneakily before the game. It was all a bit of fun and you got to go to places you would never have seen before. Trips to Belfast often included free time before the return journey, which could be a bit boring when you had no money in your pocket and had to traipse around the city centre for a couple of hours. Some of the boys from the First XV would repair to a local hostelry for a couple of beers, which we found rather daring. It could be a very long day as we left home around 7:30 am for the 8:00 am train and returned home about 5:00 pm. That was Saturday well enough accounted for as Saturday nights were still pretty much spent at home.

CHURCH AND SCOUTS

I remained a member of the choir, singing at the midweek service and twice on Sundays interspersed with weddings – for which we were paid around half a crown, a very welcome addition to the small amount of pocket money I received – and funerals. Latterly the choirboys began to get paid for their services which was a welcome supplement to my spending power, increasing it by perhaps two shillings a week.

Beyond school and choir, scouting began to take up more and more of my time. The transition from being a Cub to becoming a Scout involved some kind of ritual. It escapes my memory but no doubt required me to swear undying loyalty to God and the Queen, and an upgrading of uniform. We met on Friday nights in the Craig Hall on Infirmary Road and for two hours we learnt how to survive in the great outdoors and everything which would have been vital for a young man to know if he was destined to serve his country somewhere in the British Empire in the early years of the twentieth century. I learned how to use flags for semaphore and tried to get a grasp of Morse Code which, given it was decades before mobile phones, was not an unreasonable skill to have at one's disposal. But above all, we learned about camping.

My first camp was to a field on a farm near Eglinton, along with all the other Scout troops in the city. This annual event was in fact a competition for the right to fly the Anderson Flag at your weekly meetings. We arrived on Friday evening and were to stay until Sunday afternoon. After being shown to our site we began to set up. Scout camps are incredibly sophisticated constructions, it wasn't just a question of pitching a tent, you had to consider where to put your kitchen and most importantly of all the location of the latrine, preferably as far from the kitchen as possible. Our performance in all our activities was of course being monitored and marked. We were unsuccessful in our efforts to win the flag.

Our summer camp that year was held at Marble Hill in north-west Donegal, at a site not far from the beach. We travelled by public service on the Londonderry and Lough Swilly bus, which was an adventure in itself. On arrival we walked from the main road to the campsite, a distance of about half a mile, lugging our equipment with us. Some of the older members of the troop had preceded us and taken most of the heavy stuff with them. The rest of the day was spent pitching tents and setting up our kitchen, as each patrol had to construct its own kitchen and prepare its own meals. Cooking was done on an open fire using billycans. The kitchen was quite an elaborate affair with a dresser, a dining table, and a washing area, all constructed from wooden staves gathered from the local woods.

The spot was close to a caravan site which at the time had about three quite antiquated vans on it. (The same area today has hundreds of caravans spread across it.) Most of the people we encountered were local smallholders trying to earn a living from the land. From morning to night our day was packed with activities, ranging from gathering wood for cooking, tidying the tent for inspection, games on the beach, and singing round the campfire at night. Each member of the patrol took a turn at cooking so our diet was fairly limited and at times culinary skills were in short supply, but nobody died and some learned that they were much more able than they had thought.

I have two striking memories from that camp. Firstly, the nighttime hike, a trip of around four miles in the dark through fields and narrow farm tracks. It was quite scary, so much so that we cheated: as soon as we found a hedge that would shelter us from the wind we lay down, allowed an appropriate length of time to pass, then took a shortcut to bring us onto the return route. We brazened out the questions of our leaders who, since they are now no longer with us, will not be offended by this admission. The second memory was sleeping in a tree in the woods. We spent all day preparing our treehouse with branches and ferns and as night fell, we made ourselves comfortable in our sleeping bags and tried to fall asleep. It was a waste of time. No amount of twisting or turning could make me comfortable, there was so much wriggling around that I felt the need to lash myself to the tree. It was to no avail – about 2:00 am I gave up, clambered down the tree and made my way back to my tent. My companion was made of sterner stuff and after spending the full night up the tree, he arrived back in camp just as the rashers were hitting the pan for breakfast.

The nearest population centre to our campsite was the village of Dunfanaghy, situated about three miles distant. We were allowed into town on a couple of occasions; I remember being fascinated by the phone boxes and my inability to make them work. I also was struck by the antiquity of everything. I bought some souvenirs in a shop which had, for a counter, two upturned oil drums with a plank between them. The plank was covered in a rather handsome cloth with shamrocks embroidered along the edge. When you visit the town today it bears no comparison with how it was in the early sixties. Eventually we packed up camp and headed for home. The older Scouts who had cycled down set off somewhat sooner, we waited for the bus to bring us back. Imagine our surprise as we were passing through Creeslough to catch a glimpse of our fellow Scouts standing outside a pub, cycles propped against the wall, with a bottle of stout and a cigarette in hand relaxing in the afternoon sun. I still don't know how that story ended.

My second summer camp was a much grander affair. We went to Powerscourt, near Enniskerry in County Wicklow, just south of Dublin. We travelled from the GNR station at the foot of John Street. When I set off, I was not aware of the enormity of the journey which lay ahead of me – I thought it would be like a trip to Belfast. Not a bit of it. We seemed to trundle along at no miles an hour until five hours later we arrived in Dublin, having passed through parts of Ireland I had never heard of. From Dublin we went by bus to our campsite which I must admit was pretty impressive, set in beautiful parkland in the middle of the Powerscourt Estate.

During our stay at Powerscourt we had time for a day trip to Dublin. As part of our sightseeing we visited Nelson's Column, which of course no longer exists having been forcibly removed by the IRA in 1966. I think we made our way up to the viewing platform but I can't be sure. We also undertook a rather lengthy hike to the top of Sugarloaf Mountain, from the summit of which we were instructed to appreciate the view. During the course of the camp we also met other Scouts from exotic locations such as Carlow, of which we had never heard. They were equally as ignorant as to where we came from. We also visited Powerscourt House which, in all honesty, we were far too young to appreciate.

This was the camp where I first encountered 'blanket tossing', a kind of rite of passage for younger Scouts. Basically, it involved being put in a blanket held by your fellow Scouts and tossed high into the air, maybe to a height of twenty feet or so. It was all a bit terrifying but exhilarating too. It required a lot of faith in your brother Scouts and an ability to see beyond the potential hazards involved. I very much doubt it would be allowed nowadays.

My other lasting memory of our time in Powerscourt was the afternoon I looked over my shoulder to see my mother and father strolling towards our tents. Apparently they had set out for one of their Saturday adventures and on a whim had decided they should head to Dublin and surprise their son. I most certainly was surprised and I think my fellow Scouts were astonished at the perceived lunacy of the Thatchers. Anyway, I remember we had a great afternoon and visited the famous waterfall in the grounds of the Powerscourt Estate before they took their leave and set off on the five-hour return journey. I notice that today you need to book and pay to visit this attraction. Rather a shame.

BONNIE SCOTLAND

That summer marked another watershed moment in my life. I will never know for sure the exact details but I believe my father had become somewhat concerned about the amount of time my mother was devoting to caring for my grandmother, and as a solution had been trying to find employment elsewhere. I expect that somewhere along the line I was asked my opinion on the matter but I'm not sure I actually had one. To cut a longish story short my father had organised a transfer to a Ministry of Defence base in Beith, a small town in Ayrshire. Almost before I had time to digest this notion, I found myself packing up and transferring myself to a new life in Scotland.

So off we went to Beith, which was about twenty miles from the centre of Glasgow. I have no recollection of how we got to Beith but I presume we travelled to Glasgow on The Laird's Loch out of Derry. The Laird's Loch was principally a cattle boat, which carried passengers as an afterthought. It most certainly made no pretence at luxury – most of its attempt at customer service seemed to be directed at the bar, which every time I travelled on it appeared to do a roaring trade. Indeed, there was probably as much roaring in the bar as there was in the hold where the cattle were penned. On arriving in Glasgow, my mother and I made our way by train to Beith.

My father, who had already begun working and had acquired somewhere for us to live, led us to a flat on the second floor of a two-storey terraced house in Grahamfield Place, just beside the railway station and a few yards from a large, disused factory for whose workers I believe the dwellings had been constructed. It was a two-bedroomed dwelling without an indoor bathroom or toilet; the toilet was a shared facility found down two flights of stairs in the backyard, where there was also a communal green and washhouse for laundry days. This came as a bit of a shock to the system but I had some experience of al-fresco toilet facilities from staying at Creevagh, where a bathroom had only recently been installed. I remember our neighbours on the landing were a young couple and very agreeable.

So, everything was in place, the only remaining hurdle was school. I had been signed up to attend the local equivalent of Foyle, which was called Spiers Academy. It was located on the outskirts of town in its own grounds in a rather splendid building, with of all things a bell tower which was one hundred feet high, pretty impressive! It was a walk of ten to fifteen minutes from home. So bright and early in mid-August 1962, off I went appropriately attired in whatever the uniform was, somewhat apprehensive but determined to deal with whatever outrageous fortune had to offer.

Fortune proved to be a little more outrageous than I had anticipated. No one, least of all me, had grasped that the education system in Scotland bore only a passing resemblance to the model in Northern Ireland. The subjects remained the same, or bore the same names, but the levels of attainment did not. Since I had left Second Year it was naturally assumed that I would fit straight into Third Year in the Scottish system, alas this proved not to be. Also, since I had started secondary school a year early due to a July birthday, I found myself in classes with pupils who were two years older than me. It was very unsettling and I spent a good deal of time during the first few days sobbing uncontrollably. Luckily it was a co-educational establishment and some of the girls treated me with a certain degree of sympathy. After a lot of tears and discussion with the school management it was decided that I should really be in Second Year. So, after a false start things began to settle down, and before long I was more than able to cope with the new regime.

One of the first things I had to understand was that all of a sudden I was a 'Paddy'. No amount of explanation could make my new schoolmates understand that I was British, that Northern Ireland was an integral part of the United Kingdom and that I therefore did not qualify as a 'Paddy' and that furthermore, since my father was English, I could only qualify at most as half a 'Paddy'. They would have none of it, so for the first time in my life, in the town of Beith, I became a Paddy and would remain so throughout my sojourn in the land of 'Jocks'.

After a few weeks I began to settle in. Luckily Spiers was a rugby-playing school and I was fortunate enough to make it into the team and thus acquire a certain number of acquaintances. It was also through rugby that I was to make my best friend during my time in Scotland. We were changing after games – Spiers had the luxury of having showers – and this boy was giving me a hard time. I finally snapped and lashed out to punch him on the shoulder – he moved and my punch landed on his nose, drawing blood. There was a bit of a hush then Lewis, for so he was called, drew himself up, wiped his nose and laughed. We became firm pals, so much so that someone wrote a poem about us which appeared in the school magazine. My reputation as a true Paddy rose.

Life in Beith was pretty humdrum: school Monday to Friday, rugby on Saturday, staying at home on Sunday. Church seemed to fall into abeyance, we went once to the Episcopalian Church of Scotland in nearby Paisley but were ignored and never went back. I was relieved since it was quite an expedition by bus and foot, we had no car at that stage. Things began to pick up as I made more friends from school. Beith had a good cinema which showed all the most recent releases plus some not-quite-so-new films and we became regulars on a Saturday night. It was there that I saw The Loneliness of The Long-Distance Runner, Saturday Night and Sunday Morning, This Sporting Life, A Kind of Loving, and so forth. I don't think we were aware of their significance but they brightened up otherwise quiet Saturday nights. If we had sufficient cash left we finished the evening with tuppence-worth of chips for the walk home.

As time wore on, I began to feel somewhat at home in Scotland. I even managed to venture into Glasgow city centre on some Saturday mornings. At that time Glasgow still had a fierce reputation for violence so I was careful never to stray into the backstreets. It was also the beginning of the Swinging Sixties and the rise of popular music. We had no record player so this kind of passed me by, although I recall going to one of the big stores just to hear early Beatles songs playing in their record department, I remember thinking that I didn't particularly like them and they would more than likely be a flash in the pan. On its way into Glasgow the bus from Beith would pass in front of Ibrox Stadium, home of Glasgow Rangers, and I without fail would get an earlier bus if it was near match time. Rather cowardly, I know, but I've been blessed with a gift for avoiding trouble at almost all costs.

Soon it was almost Christmas and a decision was taken to return home for the festivities. My father had to work so it was just my mother and I who boarded the Laird's Loch for Derry. Being so close to Christmas the boat was packed with exiles making their way home to far-flung towns and villages of Donegal. Unfortunately, celebrations for some had begun early and soon, due to a mixture of seasickness and alcohol, the floor of the ship was awash with vomit which rushed to and fro with the rhythm of the waves. We found a quiet spot, kept our counsel and hoped for dawn.

The worst part of the passage was passing Rathlin Island, where it always seemed to get rough, but soon we were in the shelter of Lough Foyle. I never quite understood why it took so long to travel from Greencastle to Derry – it would have been quicker to get off and walk. Even getting from Culmore to the Quay in Derry, a distance of no more than a couple of miles, must have taken an hour. It was definitely an unforgettable voyage but who doesn't like getting home for Christmas? Time flew and it didn't seem long before it was time to board the old Laird's Loch once more and settle back into life in Scotland.

The Five Nations rugby internationals were the main source of excitement in the winter months. The school organised a bus to take us to Murrayfield in Edinburgh to see our heroes. It was quite an excursion, a drive of maybe three hours in those days before motorways, necessitating a packed lunch and a flask of piping-hot soup to be consumed on the journey and a few shillings to spend at the ground. I was a staunch supporter of the Scottish team, except of course when they played Ireland when I stood firmly with the men in green. It is fascinating to recall how amateurish the whole set up was compared to today's super grounds. We stood on an earth embankment and the facilities in the ground didn't bear thinking about. Primitive doesn't quite describe it. But it was fun and a day out with your friends could only be good.

All things considered, life was beginning to settle down. About six months after our arrival we seemed to have gathered up enough funds to install a bathroom in our flat. A chunk of the sitting room and a wee bit of the kitchen were appropriated to make room for the new facilities. After several months of washing in a bucket in front of the fire I was delighted with the luxury of a hot bath. It was such a success that the neighbours followed suit and installed one in their own flat.

Winter also brought the fun of the fair to Beith. I had never experienced anything like it, the closest I might have come were the swing-boats which came to Moville in the summer season. The fair was brilliant and seemed to have everything but it was expensive. If you turned up with two shillings or even half a crown you needed to be very judicious. Your funds could be spent in the twinkling of an eye but with careful husbandry could stretch over an hour, or maybe two. Either way, the fair was still there the next night. I'm sure parents and relatives throughout the town were pestered for spare coppers on a daily basis. Then, all of a sudden, it was gone and we were back to a diet of school and odd trips to the cinema.

One other event I remember with some pleasure was a school trip to the Isle of Arran, a fairly large island in The Firth of Clyde. I have no idea what the pretext for the excursion was but a group of around forty of us set off for a weekend on Arran. It really was an adventure. We took the steamer from Ardrossan which after a couple of hours landed us on the island at its main port Brodick, whence we walked several miles to the youth hostel which was to be our base, no doubt chosen for its remoteness. I remember that we behaved just as all children seem to do on school trips: we slept very little and annoyed our teachers no end.

In revenge, they got us up at cock crow and after breakfast led us off on an all-day hike. We were to climb Goatfell, the highest mountain on the island, rising to a height of almost three thousand feet. We were young and able and enjoyed the walk. I marvel at the lack of preparation we had for the trek, nowadays we would have spent hours getting organised and ages on health and safety. We skipped along the narrow paths in our ordinary shoes paying little attention to the perilous drops on either side of us as we made our way towards the summit. Had anyone slipped I'm sure they would have rolled many hundreds of feet down the precipitous scree slopes. No one was hurt beyond the acquisition of a few blisters and if the teachers had hoped we would be exhausted and instantly fall into a deep sleep when our heads hit the pillow, I'm afraid they were disappointed. I have never returned to Arran but every time I drive up the coast to Glasgow and look across to the island, with its peaks standing clear in the bright afternoon sun, memories of those few days come flooding back.

During my first summer in Scotland, my mother had the brilliant idea that I could join up with my friends in Christ Church Scouts, who were having their summer camp at Auchengillan not far from Loch Lomond. I met the advance party of half a dozen Scouts as they disembarked from The Laird's Loch in Glasgow docks. After loading the camping gear onto an open-topped lorry and scrambling on to it ourselves, we set off through Glasgow for the campsite. The job of the advance party was to set up camp and begin pitching tents before the rest of the troop arrived the next day. The party consisted of some of the older Scouts and they were a little taken aback to be lumbered with thirteen-year-old me. They had plans for an evening out and were determined to proceed with them despite my presence. They were going into Glasgow and I was going with them.

The problem was that I was only equipped with scouting gear so had to be trigged out in civilian clothing, but my colleagues were all a few years older and several inches taller. Scouts are noted for their ingenuity and so it was that I boarded the bus for Glasgow in borrowed clothes, hastily stitched up and cleverly folded so they at least appeared to fit. The night out was a bit of a damp squib, Glasgow hostelries were much less receptive to underage customers than those at home might have been, especially with a thirteen-year-old wearing strange clothing in tow. We eventually went to the cinema to see a film of little merit. The rest of the camp was brilliant. As usual my mother and father made an unannounced visit, which once again I really appreciated. I enjoyed being with my friends again and was a bit homesick when the time came to say goodbye as they headed home to Derry.

As the school year drew to a close I realised that I was a little more settled and was coming to grips with the different system of education. Whilst Art continued to be one of my weakest subjects, it also proved witness to one of my great sporting feats. The Art Room was a large, dedicated space with paintings and sculpture dotted around the walls. We sat at individual desks which in the old-fashioned way still had little inkpots sat in an opening in the desk. As usual, Art didn't inspire the best of behaviour and one classmate was especially difficult. On this day he was in a particularly foul mood and was being remarkably obnoxious. To cut a long story short he picked up an inkwell and hurled it as hard as he could towards the teacher, who had her back turned to him. I caught sight of it at the very last second, stuck my hand out and snatched it out of the air, making a catch that would have graced a test match at Lords. Disaster was averted, no one bar a couple of classmates noticed what had happened, and life went on. A few years later I discovered that the thrower of the inkwell had been sent to borstal as the result of an armed robbery. I am glad our paths never crossed again.

BACK ON THE FARM

In the end-of-year examinations I had acquitted myself reasonably well, much to my relief. When the school holidays finally arrived I was sent home to Granny and Granda in Nicholson Terrace, where I met up with my friends once again. It wasn't long however before I found myself back on the farm. By this time I had learned how to drive a tractor, although my activities were confined to working in the fields. Jobs which required a tractor to be driven up and down a field to facilitate the spreading of manure (colloquially referred to as 'scaling dung') or the lifting of sacks dotted across a field, were deemed within my level of competence.

I was also working on my car driving. My principal drawback was the shortness of my legs but with the judicious placement of a cushion I was soon able to master first and reverse gears in the car, moving slowly across the yard when no one was looking. My driving ability was rather suddenly put to the test in an unexpected way. I was out with one of the cousins looking at animals when we were involved in a collision with another car. For some reason the police were called and after a good deal of sitting around, accompanied by bouts of shouting and accusations, the police decided the cousin would go with them to the station to make a statement. I was allegedly to sit in the car and await the arrival of somebody to drive it, and me, home. Unbeknown to the police it had been decided that I, aged thirteen, would drive the car back.

Having allowed a suitable amount of time to elapse, I propped myself up on a cushion and set off. I was no mug, I knew exactly how to proceed. The accident had happened on the road to Carrigans and I knew that if I took the right options I could do most of the trip on back roads and private roads. There was one major hurdle to overcome: the car had its gearshift on the steering column and I had no experience of using it. Notwithstanding, off I went: down the Moss Road, along to the entrance to Lynn's farm, up the private lane to the upper road and home to Creevagh. On the whole journey of about three miles I only encountered one oncoming vehicle, which I flew past without any difficulty. No one in Creevagh noticed my arrival and when my cousin finally got home I was told in no uncertain terms to keep my mouth shut! My first trip in a car with me at the wheel had ended without mishap.

School holidays in Scotland are shorter than the ones enjoyed in Northern Ireland, so I was a bit put out when I was bundled back to Beith in id-August to resume my studies. Moving into Year Three was a big deal, as you had to choose the subjects you intended to study for the equivalent of O-levels. I hadn't a clue. I liked Geography, indeed when I did my last exams at Foyle I had finished top in the subject. I had done so well that the teacher Mr Leclerc had re-marked my paper because he was taken aback, but he had to grin and bear it.

In Scotland Geography turned into Historical Geography. I wasn't quite so taken with it but it has left me with a sound grasp of the early colonial history and geography of Canada, which was what the syllabus offered, perhaps explained by the enormous numbers of Scots who emigrated to Canada during its formative years. I also somehow continued to study General Science, which I hated, and began to study German, which I rather liked due perhaps to a young and enthusiastic teacher. My academic career was off to a shaky start. I had given little thought to the subjects I was going to study and the one I really had my heart set on, Geography, was unavailable.

During my stay in Scotland I had two unique experiences, one of which was distinctly unpleasant. At the back of Grahamfield Place there was a green which was used to dry washing during the summer months. Being a green it had grass, and it was the shared duty of the occupants to keep things looking shipshape. It was one of my chores to mow the green as and when appropriate. One day the communal mower seemed more reluctant than ever to trim the grass, so I took it upon myself to sharpen the blades. I found my father's whetstone in his toolbox and set to. When I felt the blades were sufficiently sharp I spun them round and felt the edge of the spinning blades with my finger, just to check how sharp they actually were. Just sharp enough to leave the end of the middle finger on my right hand dangling, attached to the rest of me by skin and a tiny bit of flesh!

As you might imagine, I was a little stunned. Holding the remains of my finger in my left hand I ran upstairs to my mother who quickly assessed the situation. The hospital was at least an hour away by bus, not to mention waiting times in the Casualty Department, so the only answer was to do the repairs at home. Out came the iodine and sticking plaster and in the twinkling of an eye, the bleeding was stopped and the finger reattached with the aforementioned plaster. Since no bones had been broken the flesh soon grew back, but to this day there is still a little lump of excess flesh which protrudes slightly at the top of the finger. One unexpected bonus to arise from this piece of foolishness was that during the cricket season I was able to give the ball a little more of a tweak whilst bowling, improving my average no end.

The second experience happened on a rather damp and chilly autumn evening. Mother and I were sitting quietly watching television when we heard sirens and a fire engine passed close by. Naturally, I went out to investigate. The disused factory at the top of our street had caught fire and flames and smoke were billowing from the building. Being naturally inquisitive I made my way up towards the fire. Beith only had a volunteer fire brigade, with one appliance and perhaps half a dozen volunteers. As this was obviously a major fire I suddenly found myself having a hose thrust into my hand and being instructed to point the jet at a certain point of the building. For about ten minutes I was a firefighter aged thirteen, then the professionals arrived from the neighbouring village and I was relieved of my duties and sent to stand behind the cordon which had been established by the police. When I eventually made my way home I was severely scolded by my mother but it was worth it, if only for the story I had to tell in school the next day. Naturally I was careful not to wash too thoroughly next morning so I still had the reek of smoke about me to add veracity to the tale, which I was eager to share with my friends.

As the second Christmas in Scotland approached, I was deemed old enough to travel by myself. We had acquired a car by this time, a Morris Estate with a wooden frame known I think as a 'Traveller', so I was driven to the terminal in Glasgow and met by someone at Aldergrove. I stayed in Nicholson Terrace, had quite a good Christmas with various relatives, and as soon as it was over I flew back to Glasgow. The only thing that stands out from this trip was that on the return journey I seemed to have more possessions than I brought with me. I recall going up the steps to the aircraft wearing two raincoats and a sports jacket looking for all the world like a barrage balloon. The flight ended without a hitch, I was collected at Glasgow airport, and before you could say Jack Robinson I was back at school and life resumed its daily routine.

Many years later, I discovered that as I was enjoying Derry with all the fun and food of the festive season, money was so tight in the Thatcher household that Mum and Dad were sitting down to a tin of chicken soup for their Christmas dinner. Changes however were afoot. I hadn't noticed anything particularly different during my trip home but Granny's illness had begun to worsen and she was finding life very difficult to manage, especially as mobility was concerned. Not long after the start of the new school term it was announced that we were leaving Scotland and going back home to look after Granny. All that I could think was: How would this work?

During our stay in Beith I had rediscovered my love of pets and had worked my way through a range of small animals. I began with a hamster whose nocturnal activities on his treadmill kept the whole house awake. I moved on to terrapins that didn't seem to like us much and expired quite rapidly. Next came a salamander, which was quite good fun but he escaped one night and despite a rigorous search remained at large for months, turning up about ten weeks later looking forlorn and shrivelled due to dehydration. He stayed for a while but then he also expired. Finally, I settled on goldfish, which thrived in a tank in my bedroom. Therein lay the problem: how would these fish manage to get back to Derry? The easiest solution would have been to flush them down the toilet, but my father was nothing if not compassionate, so a plan was devised to transport them in their tank in the back of the Morris Traveller. The task was accomplished with not too much difficulty, although it did raise some eyebrows amongst officials when we checked in at Stranraer.

HOME TO DERRY

And so in the month of February I relinquished my soubriquet of Paddy and became plain Ken once again. As soon as I returned to Foyle, the system conspired to mess me up for the second time. Having just about caught up with the Scottish education syllabus, I was once again cast adrift in the Northern Irish one, from frying pan to fire in no uncertain terms. It most certainly didn't help that all this upheaval was taking place in February, right in the middle of the school year. Nothing seemed to coincide, certainly not Maths or English which was rather disconcerting.

I also had to be squeezed back into the Foyle way. The O-level settings in Foyle insisted that you were either a mathematician, a scientist, or 'other', other meaning vaguely 'literary'. I was neither of the first two so I was placed in 4L. Unfortunately, 4L lent itself to misfits, those neither mathematically inclined, nor overly interested in science and not always of a literary bent. I was more than able to fit in. All my previous classmates seemed to have slotted into the other two sets, so I had to establish another circle of friends, which I did without too much trouble. Whilst we clicked, we did so in the worst possible way. We took pleasure in being awkward, going out of our way to make life difficult for our teachers.

I was studying Latin, German and French and was dropped into the middle of a History syllabus which did nothing for me. What remote interest might I have in the history of the USA? Cowboys and Indians might have elicited some interest, with a distinct leaning towards the indigenous people; beyond that, nothing. Maths and English were once again different specifications … there was not a lesson in which I felt at home. In the course of my first French lesson back in Foyle, the teacher said to me: 'There was a boy called Thatcher who left a couple of years ago, are you related to him in any way?' On hearing me reply in the affirmative, I could tell by his crestfallen look that all was not well. This was most definitely not an auspicious start to my new academic career.

School apart, I had no difficulty in reintegrating with my old friends. Life took on its usual round but I was now a teenager and it was the sixties, so things were bound to be different, were they not? One thing which was incontrovertibly different was my voice. It had broken and there was no way I was able to continue to sing in the choir, but Christ Church continued to play a significant role in my social life. I rejoined the Scouts, perhaps with less enthusiasm than before, and became a member of the Youth Club which met regularly during the year. Other social activities included going to the cinema and spending too much time in Yannerelli's coffee bar. Yannerelli's on the Strand Road was the cool place to be seen in the early to mid-sixties; it had a jukebox with all the latest music and it had girls, who were, to my surprise, becoming a more attractive diversion in my life. I'd known about girls while living in Scotland, having been in a co-educational school, but all of a sudden they had taken on a more alluring quality which was at once charming yet disconcerting.

I digress. My performance at school was becoming more and more alarming – I was in a class with people who were intelligent but who were, for the most part, disenchanted with education. With one or two exceptions they were signed up to complete their O-levels and then they were off to work. Higher education was deemed appropriate for a very few of my colleagues, perhaps those wishing to become doctors or academics. Most jobs in the sixties could be achieved through apprenticeships or training as you worked – university was considered a luxury by most families and an expensive luxury at that. Even though in those heady days you were given a grant to study at third level, it was impossible to complete the course without some financial help from parents.

I can say with confidence that there was not a single subject which I found motivating. The only subject I really enjoyed, Geography, was no longer accessible due to my change of curriculum. My situation was not helped by having some inexperienced teachers who were not capable of dealing with pupils who refused point blank to cooperate. (I include myself in that category.) We had two teachers who were Oxbridge graduates who hadn't a notion how to deal with reluctant learners; one offered violence, the other indifference.

The former tried to interest us in History, he taught us in Room 6 in the prefabricated huts left over from the school's occupation by the military during the war. The situation of these rooms was such that they were slightly isolated from the rest of the building and therefore not quite so strictly supervised. Room 6 was the middle of three rooms and accessed from a short corridor to the left of the building. The teacher worked from a low dais at the front of the room and we sat in rows in front of him. I sat in the back row, naturally. During the course of lessons, we would take it in turns to quietly jump out of the window at the end of our row and make our way back round to the door, knock, apologise for being late and resume our seat. The poor man must have thought he had a class of fifty, there were so many late arrivals.

One day it all became too much for him. Someone did genuinely arrive late – he had been seeing the headmaster – and the teacher snapped and began thumping the boy with his fists. He had chosen the wrong moment. The boy took umbrage at this treatment and began to fight back. Classroom furniture was raised and things began to look a bit scary but order was eventually restored. However, that teacher was shortly to be replaced and was never seen or heard of again. I look back with some sorrow on that episode in my education.

The room next door was occupied by one of the Maths teachers; when things became a little too raucous in Room 6 he would intervene and take half a dozen of the worst offenders to sit at the back of his class.

More often than not I was one of the chosen few. There was always a hint of violence underlying the maintenance of discipline, probably in all schools at this time, and I was to witness an example of this whilst sitting at the back of this classroom. Geometry was the theme of the lesson and the teacher was questioning his young charges on the names and properties of geometric shapes. One pupil, when asked the name of a five-sided shape, was struck dumb. At the time I was sure he knew the answer but was so tense he was unable to get the word out. In order to help, the teacher prompted him with the first syllable of the word, which he repeated more than once. With a smile the pupil responded to his prompt. He misheard 'Poly', and hearing 'Polly', quick as a flash replied 'put the kettle on', with a broad smile of relief crossing his face. It didn't last: the teacher failed to see the funny side of this retort and violence ensued. Fortunately, no lasting damage was done and said pupil went on to distinguish himself in the field of education.

Latin was the other subject in which we were privileged to be taught by an Oxbridge graduate. He was faced by a crowd of boys who had no more interest in Latin than the man in the moon. Chaos reigned and he had no chance, but he persevered. He tried to woo us by translating 'Yellow Submarine' by The Beatles into Latin and getting us to sing it whilst he accompanied us on his guitar. We acknowledged that he was trying but we proved to be even more trying. If memory serves me, when the results were published fewer than half a dozen managed a pass. School got its revenge – next term an extra class was organised for those who had deigned to fail and under the severe supervision of a more experienced teacher, we all performed respectably in our resit. We did at one stage show a certain amount of respect or compassion for Tom, for that was his name. He had fallen ill and was hospitalised so the class clubbed together, bought a couple of packets of his favourite cigarettes, and went to visit him in hospital. Tom was somewhat overcome when half a dozen of us arrived, whether with pleasure or embarrassment I was never sure. He continued to teach at Foyle for some years and I know that tales of Mr Dunn and his rather esoteric car abound amongst pupils of that era.

SNOOKERED

Life beyond school changed little. Perhaps we ventured 'up the town' a bit more often, though what we did when we got there didn't add up to a lot. I had also become quite good at smoking, so scraping enough cash together to fund this habit took a bit of ingenuity. Gathering and returning refundable empty bottles was one method and of course we still managed to do odd jobs in the All Cash Stores for a few pence.

We also discovered the docks. Derry was still quite a busy port and foreign boats were fairly frequent visitors. We discovered that sailors would often throw us a packet of cigarettes if we begged sufficiently or gave them helpful hints on which locations were most worth a visit, usually bars and dancehalls. Derry was still an important military establishment in the sixties with warships from NATO countries berthed along the quay, mostly frigates, destroyers and sometimes submarines, stretching from the Guildhall to the old graving dock, sometimes two abreast.

Commercially the docks were also a hive of activity, with boats discharging coal or grain and being loaded with cattle or potatoes. The light railway tracks, which were still in situ until the quayside was redeveloped, permitted goods to be moved in trucks from down the graving dock at Meadowbank and upriver as far as the GNR station at the end of the Craigavon Bridge. Sometimes, at night, we would climb into these freight trucks to shelter from the cold or to share a quick cigarette. Once we tried to push a truck along its track but that drew the wrath of the Harbour Police, the 'Dock Cornies', who chased us off the docks and into the Strand Road, where their jurisdiction ended.

I was becoming familiar with other new entertainments as well. I had become interested in snooker, which I played in the GOH Hall, a rather grand name for a couple of seedy rooms accessed by a series of stairs leading to the top storey of houses at the corner of Clarendon Street and Strand Road. I have never found out what GOH stood for – there was a suggestion it was connected to the Hibernians but I could never prove it. It was certainly a pretty low dive but you could get a game quite quickly and that was all we were interested in. It was also pretty much out of bounds for protestants but that didn't seem to matter too much in the mid-sixties. Several of us would go in after school wearing our Foyle blazers without exciting too much comment. I became so much of a regular in the GOH that I acquired a nickname. I became known as 'Beatle', presumably because my hair was a little long and also because I apparently bore a slight resemblance to Paul McCartney, although I could never see it myself. That was sort of the way things were at the time.

Snooker began to occupy more and more of my spare time and I became known in many of the clubs in the city. It's astonishing to think how many there were: I played in The Presbyterian Working Men's Institute overlooking the Diamond, the Church of Ireland Young Men's Club in Ferryquay Street, the A O H in Foyle Street, The Forester's Hall in Magazine Street, and even graced the Masonic Hall and The Catholic Club with my presence. I was anything but discriminating in pursuit of snooker. I played so much I ought to have become rather a good player, unfortunately I was usually almost average. On the positive side I got acquainted with a broad spectrum of the local snooker-playing population and got to know how the other half lived, so to speak.

THE CYCLIST

At the end of Fourth Year at Foyle I decided that it would be good to earn some money and so began actively seeking work, as they used to say, in 'The Bru'. The Labour Exchange was full of people much more worthy of employment than me, but I was lucky and as a result of my casual employment in our local shop, I was taken on by 'The All Cash Stores' as a delivery boy. I was to start as soon as the school holidays began. My first placement was at the shop on Academy Road, which meant getting to work was pretty easy. If I wanted to, I could stay in bed until 8:50 am and still be five minutes early, as all I had to do was walk across the street and into the shop.

Every branch of 'The Cash Stores' had a delivery boy but some locations were much easier than others. The Academy Road shop was halfway up a quite steep hill, so most deliveries were either up or down, necessitating good load planning, strong leg muscles, and a reliable set of brakes. Knowing the area meant that I could usually plan my itinerary to avoid too many strenuous climbs in the course of the day. Generally, it was good fun and the customers were usually quite appreciative of your efforts, every so often you might get a few pence as a tip. Most of the message boys were full-time employees and therefore were entitled to holidays. This meant that I could be moved from one branch to another to cover their absence. My first transfer was to the branch on Strand Road, close to the junction with the Buncrana Road. I was pleased as it was basically flat terrain but had forgotten that it was uphill to Belmont, where new houses were being built, and that Culmore Road, although not densely populated, was also uphill.

The demographics of the areas were interesting. Culmore Road would have been populated by more affluent customers, who it transpired were much less likely to be generous with their tips and much more ready to complain if there was any delay in their order. I subsequently worked in the branches on the Lecky Road and also on Bishop Street Without. The latter was even hillier than Academy Road, nowhere was on the level. The scariest street I ever had to deliver groceries on was Howard Street; I learned very quickly that it was best negotiated on foot, pushing the message bike.

I enjoyed the few weeks I spent round Bishop Street, the people were very friendly and would frequently invite you in for a cup of tea or a chat. Almost every house I called at in the area would have a photograph of J.F.K. hung prominently on the wall, next to an image of The Sacred Heart and of course a picture of his Holiness John Paul XXIII or, if they were up to date, Pope Paul VI. What I wasn't prepared for was when on the Twelfth of July, as I went through a house to the kitchen to unpack the groceries, the television was blaring out music from marching bands on parade in Belfast, celebrating King Billy's victory at The Boyne in 1690. I was told that the lady in question just loved the pageantry of it all. I said very little and accepted the few coppers' tip. Not once in the course of that summer did I hear a word that might be construed as sectarian or bitter, regardless of what part of town I was required to work.

I must say I enjoyed my time as a message boy, despite the vicissitudes of the weather and the occasional barking dog which might attack the bike. (I kept a stick to hand to deal with that.) What I liked most was the brown envelope which appeared every week containing two one-pound notes and six shillings, my first official wage. No doubt I ought to have handed it over to my mother like a dutiful son, but she didn't ask so I didn't offer. Two pounds in 1964 was a fair sum – you could get into the pictures for two shillings. If you were interested you could sit in The Rainbow Cafe in Waterloo Place, The Dolphin, originally in Sackville Street latterly on the Strand Road, or The Leprechaun, although it was a little more sedate and frequented by ladies of a certain age who talked very politely and ate their scones with a great sense of decorum. These ladies were horrified one day when they saw my friends and I buy an apple tart each from the bakery at the front of 'The Lep', take it to a table and after ordering cups of tea to keep us legal, set to. Each of us had no difficulty in polishing off our purchases. Next time we stopped by there was a sign declaring that any food bought in the bakery was not to be consumed on the premises. Luckily there were at least half a dozen other cafés where you could sit chatting for ages and if you were fortunate, catch the eye of some girl or another. All for the price of a cup of coffee, which was less than a shilling.

O-LEVELS

I began my Fifth Year in Foyle with as little knowledge of what lay ahead or its importance as of the man in the moon. I was still suffering from the gaps in my understanding in certain subjects and had made little effort to do anything about it, the only thing I really enjoyed was sport and in particular rugby. I was still an academic year ahead of my actual age so I played for The Medallion Fifteen for two years in succession and must confess I loved it. My academic work continued to be just about par; I had no idea of what I might be aiming for or of the options open to me after the end of Fifth Year. I was rudderless and my behaviour left a lot to be desired.

Outside school I dropped out of Scouts but remained in the Youth Club. Every church in the town seemed to have a youth club, developed no doubt in an effort to keep the young off the streets and engender some kind of civic spirit in them. Church youth groups seemed to be run by young curates who still felt in touch with the younger members of the congregation. Naturally I gravitated towards the club organised by the curate at Christ Church. It took place on Sunday evenings, initially in The Craig Memorial Hall on Infirmary Road before moving to a Nissan Hut behind the old City and County Hospital, after medical facilities transferred to the Altnagelvin site.

The club was run by a succession of young curates who hoped they still had a rapport with the youth. It was not overtly religious but it was obvious that was its underlying ethos. What was available for us young people were the usual activities, such as table tennis and snooker, made all the more exciting for us by the participation of girls. Often the evening ended with a debate on social topics of the day. We were allowed to choose the topics put up for debate and, being young and thinking ourselves radical, we frequently debated such topics as free love and the importance of the church in the twentieth century. The former elicited much more audience participation than the latter; it also tested the patience of the young clergyman who had to ensure things did not get out of hand or cross the line between decency and lewdness.

One other significant event organised by the church was the Friday-night 'Hop'. What, I wondered, was a 'Hop'? I finally discovered many years later that it was defined not as the act of jumping on one foot but simply an informal dance. The hop, held in the Craig Hall, was ostensibly to raise funds for youth organisations and was eagerly anticipated by all the youth of the parish. Normally the music was provided by one of the many local groups which abounded in the mid-sixties. When Friday night arrived there was great excitement, because although it looked enormous at the time, the hall only held about two hundred people so it was important to arrive early as there was invariably a queue and not everybody would get in.

They were great events, loud, hot, and sweaty. There was no suggestion of strong drink, minerals and crisps were the only available refreshments. Sometimes things would get a bit out of hand – usually concerning differences over girls – and scuffles would break out. I clearly recall one such scuffle which took the intervention of clergy to settle. The rector, Canon Griffin, later to be Dean of St Patrick's in Dublin, reversed his watch to protect the face, waded in between the two warring factions, and succeeded in bringing the altercation to a speedy conclusion. The one and only time in my life that I was involved in such a scrap, I found myself standing with a chair held above my head, ready to bring it down on somebody's back. I paused and thought briefly of the consequences, then carefully put the chair down and walked to the other side of the hall. Thus ended my only foray into dancehall brawling.

The dance always ended at midnight and we all peacefully made our way home. Looking back, I am astonished at how much those dances in the Craig Hall were inter-denominational, which at that time was rather unusual. I used to think there must have been hundreds of dance-goers, but with hindsight it's obvious that the hall was full to bursting with only a couple of hundred at most.

The other principal leisure activity which preoccupied most teenage boys was going 'up the town'. 'Up the town' could include anywhere from the Culmore Road to the lower reaches of Carlisle Road. The Waterside remained almost out of bounds, it was considered literally a step too far. The starting point for these expeditions was for us Yanerelli's' on Strand Road. Usually we would gather there around 7:30 pm and buy a drink, which would last as long as the staff tolerated us. Generally we managed to spin out our stay until about 8:00 pm and then it was made clear that we would have to give up our table. We thought 'Yan's' was the bee's knees: nowhere else in town was considered to be so 'cool' and it did attract the finest of young ladies whose objectives, I suspect, differed very little from our own.

The object of going 'up the town' was the – usually futile – pursuit of the opposite sex. Sunday was the busiest night and the town centre would be thronged with people walking purposefully along the principal thoroughfares of the city. In good old sixties Northern Ireland nothing was open on Sunday, except of course churches. Unless you had the means and the transport to cross into Donegal – where all sorts of diversions were available, from pubs to amusement arcades and above all dancehalls – in Derry you had to make your own entertainment, and if that meant walking up and down the city streets well, so be it.

Of course, when you were 'up the town' you had to look just right. When I made my first foray into the local beau monde I believed that a black pullover and mustard-coloured tie were de rigueur; anything else you wouldn't have been seen dead in. Shortly after that it was the denim shirt with the button-down collar which became the absolute latest accessory. If you could credit it, in a town swamped by shirts, getting the right shade of denim with the appropriate collar proved quite tricky. Luckily, Doherty's boutique in Waterloo Street generally came up trumps.

As an ardent follower of fashion, I also remember buying a pair of Cuban-heeled boots, as worn by several of the most popular musicians of the day. John Lennon sported a pair on many an occasion. My mother was horrified, she just didn't get why young men would want to go out in high heels. It became the subject of bitter arguments between us. (My father rather judiciously stayed out of it.) If I wanted to wear them, I would surreptitiously put them in a bag and slip them on outside the house. One day, I couldn't find them. I searched the house to no avail. I may have left them behind when changing back to come home, I surmised. Years later, when reminiscing with my mother, she admitted that in a fit of pique she had put my precious Cuban-heeled boots into the range, where they were consumed in some kind of holy fire. I thought I looked rather well in them. Evidently, she did not.

Getting back to those endless Sunday evening peregrinations: to what end were they? Perhaps the hope of an encounter with a member of the opposite sex who might give you an encouraging smile, leading to an actual conversation and the promise of a meeting at some future date. Did that ever happen? Only once was I successful and that future meeting was a one off, a shared coffee at my expense and an unfulfilled promise to see each other again.

On another occasion I had arranged to meet a girl on a Wednesday evening outside Austin's of the Diamond at 7:30 pm. By 8:00 pm, having spent the time nonchalantly pacing to and fro, feigning interest in the displays in the shop windows, I grasped that she wasn't coming and decided to make the best of a bad job and set off home. As I passed through Guildhall Square, I could see a small crowd gathered at the front entrance to The City Hotel. Since there was a great deal of noise and screams I went to look. There, at the very front, was my alleged date, screaming her head off. Inside were The Swinging Blue Jeans, who were to play at the Embassy Ballroom that evening. The said Blue Jeans were hanging out of the hotel windows, encouraging their fans to further excess. Suddenly, a few of the girls at the front of the crowd were ushered into the hotel, amongst them my erstwhile date. I had been jilted in favour of a pop idol. I trudged home really none the worse for it; not for the last time had I been cast to one side in favour of a better option.

One other interest I developed at this stage and which has stayed with me since is card playing. I'm not sure when this passion began but I do know that when we went to that scout camp in Powerscourt, it was important that a deck of cards came with us. At first, we were very unsophisticated and played very simple games like Snap but quite quickly we developed an interest in Pontoon, which we played for matchsticks. It wasn't long before we were dragged in to playing for hard cash. We were fortunate that coins were plentiful and we were able to make wagers from a halfpenny upwards. No one was going to get rich quick but it was addictive. Behind Christ Church there was a triangle of land which in former days had been used as a putting green and an outdoor badminton court. There was also a small shed, a kind of clubhouse which had fallen into disuse and was at that time a store for all sorts of bits and pieces but importantly, a table and a few chairs. The older scouts used it as a kind of den; we decided that it would be ideal for cards. We thought we were the bee's knees, sprawled out with a cigarette, pretending we were in Las Vegas. It was all innocent fun, you were never going to win more than a shilling or lose more than sixpence.

One night we were in full session, cards on the table, the hut filled with smoke, when there was an almighty crash and the door burst open. There, framed in the doorway was the Curate, face purple with fury. I think he was expecting at the very least a band of thugs but all he got was us. We were mortified, but when he calmed down he gave us good 'eating' and left it at that. We soon found another hideaway to continue our sport. Eventually we learned how to play Poker and worse still we started to play in school, at break and lunch time. At one stage I was worried as cards seemed to consume a great deal of my life but it never got out of hand and no one ever lost too much. I vaguely hoped it might give me a better understanding of maths and probability.

And how was school going? Truth to tell, not very well. In most subjects I would have been happy to be average, but with Maths in particular I was struggling. I couldn't quite grasp the notion that you could multiply letters; numbers were difficult enough. I still hadn't recovered from the move from Scotland and didn't have the sense to admit my failings to anybody, least of all the school, not that I think school was particularly interested in my shortcomings. I was swiftly turning into a pain in the backside.

Life beyond the classroom continued on its merry way. There was still snooker, still the cinema, and a passing interest in girls, but now added to the mix was drink. I don't wish to suggest that I was a serious drinker but the excitement of an illicit drink always had a certain attraction, it was part of the ritual of growing up. Derry had never been short of pubs and we soon discovered it was possible to obtain drink from certain establishments. We were never allowed in but if we went discreetly to a side entrance we could be served with some sort of carry-out. We favoured The Fahan Bar with our custom. Its location opposite Butcher Gate made it ideal, as after the liquor was bought it could be consumed in secret up The Walls. Local wisdom had it that The Fahan blended its own concoction of wine, allegedly in a tin bath in the back yard. Two choices were available: one cost half a crown a bottle, the other three shillings and thruppence. It was rumoured that the more expensive bottle contained a higher percentage of methylated spirit. Apparently, you could tell the percentage of meths by the intensity of the cold you experienced on the back of your throat. We were lucky that our palates were more sophisticated than this and before too long we found a pub which was willing to overlook the fact that we were still only sixteen, or in my case fifteen.

Sometimes we were more adventurous and would set off with a tent, often to somewhere nearby like Portrush, where we would pitch in one of the numerous caravan parks and stay as long as funds lasted. On one occasion we were a bit more ambitious and set off for a weekend in the 'Republic', ending up doing wild camping in the hills outside Bray. We lived on sausages and tea made from water from a nearby stream. At night we sampled the delights of downtown Bray, which failed to fire our imagination. We also fell foul of some local youths who declared that 'black northerners' should stay where they belonged, fortunately we were able to shake them off.

We also spent a day in Dublin, which was still mostly intact, not yet having succumbed to the wrath of the developers' bulldozers. I didn't really have any idea of what the city had to offer us so, after a few hours trailing round shops, we headed back to our tents. After a couple of days we decided we'd had enough and on a whim we dared to hitch-hike home. That was a bit of a nightmare – it took no fewer than fifteen lifts to complete the one-hundred-and-fifty-mile journey. It might have helped if we'd had a better sense of direction or a map; setting off on the road to Belfast was probably a bit of a setback. We left at 9:00 am and just about got home by midnight. The strangest of the lifts was in a Land Rover which stopped for us just outside Omagh. We found ourselves in the company of some 'B Specials' who were just setting out on patrol. Even in those less troubled times this seemed just a wee bit scary. They took us from Omagh as far as Newtownstewart, around ten miles, which was about the average for the journey.

A REALITY CHECK

Time ticked by and soon we were into May and O-levels began. I can't remember if I took them that seriously; knowing me I assumed that things would work out. What was really occupying my mind was a job for the summer holidays. I had grown a bit too large to be a message boy but fortune smiled on me and I was lucky enough to be required on the farm. Financially this wouldn't be too rewarding but at least I wouldn't be sitting around the house scrounging for cash and getting under everyone's feet. The bucolic life kept me busy although every so often my mind would drift to exam results and their consequences. I successfully pushed these thoughts to the back of my mind.

So, the summer passed and inexorably the shadow of results day approached. For many of my colleagues this was to be the natural end to their academic life, consequently they had already made arrangements for their future and indeed some had already begun working. As usual I had made no plans whatsoever; I was trusting to luck. Results were available to collect from school so with an air of dread I made my way down Crawford Square and slowly turned into Lawrence Hill, thinking it might be for the final time.

I opened the envelope, took a deep breath, and scanned the page of results. Not quite as bad as might have been but nothing to write home about. I had done well enough to get back into school to do A-levels, the only question was: did I want to? It transpired that I didn't really know, so by default that meant that I would sign up for another two years in Foyle and study French, German and History. I didn't even stop to think where that combination might lead. That was the next couple of years taken care of and that was all that mattered as far as I was concerned. I reported my results back home and shared my decision to continue with my education. Everyone looked happy. Whether they were or not was another matter.

NOSE TO THE GRINDSTONE

So, September saw me back in the old crimson blazer treading the well-worn path down Lawrence Hill. Being in Sixth Form meant that you were supposed to be treated as much more grown up, indeed as young adults, and in truth many more activities were available to us. One of these was the Debating Society, which met on Friday evenings. We debated all the topics which were exciting the youth of that era: mostly sex, drugs, and politics. Local politics especially was beginning to interest us and we were becoming increasingly aware of world politics. We were, after all, children of the Cold War, had lived through the Cuban Crisis and were just becoming aware of the Civil Rights movement in America.

One of the most interesting facets of the Debating Society was that it allowed us to meet students from other local schools, notably the boys of St Columb's and more excitingly the girls from Thornhill. I particularly enjoyed our visits to The Convent Grammar School in Strabane, a college devoted to the education of catholic girls. There was at the time a rumour that the nuns were trying to entice young protestant boys into the embrace of young catholic girls in order to win converts to The Church of Rome. That aside, the nuns were famous for their hospitality and invariably provided a good spread after the debating was finished, plus I was more than willing to be welcomed into the embrace of any young lady regardless of their faith. On a more serious note, for many of us this would have been the first opportunity to discover what our peers from other religious persuasions were thinking. For some, it must have been a bit of an eye-opener. We began to discover that there was a growing unease in the city, mostly around the issue of housing and of course the debate about the location of Northern Ireland's second university.

One day a few friends and I were invited to Stormont by our local sitting member. I confess that I was overawed by the occasion. We were met at the front entrance to the iconic building and given the guided tour, including an appearance on the balcony which has that rather splendid view down the hill to the sprawl of Belfast lying below. We then were shown into the visitors' gallery where we listened to part of a debate before being taken to the dining room for something to eat. Whilst there we were met by our local MP who no doubt thought he was storing up potential votes for the future without having to do much work to gain them. I sat in silence as some fairly disparaging remarks were made concerning my fellow citizens' work ethic. My more emboldened colleagues felt more able to disagree with these remarks and suddenly the atmosphere turned a little more frosty. The upshot of the event was that we stayed too long at Stormont and missed the last train home but fortunately my friend's father was happy to drive up and collect us. I confess I was taken aback by the attitude of our MP towards his constituents, even if they wouldn't have voted for him in a million years.

The 'University for Derry' campaign was also gathering momentum and a motor cavalcade was organised to show that the people of the city were united in their support for the project. Foyle College decided that if students felt strongly enough they would be permitted to attend, which on reflection seems quite a progressive attitude. I'm not certain I wasn't more excited by the prospect of a day off lessons rather than by higher motives. I went to Stormont with thousands of others in a great display of solidarity but, as history shows, we were not to be winners of that battle.

In extracurricular activities I seemed to be meeting more and more people from different sides of the community, but as far as the social side of things went, life continued more or less as normal. In school my studies were making some progress and I found myself increasingly interested in literature. I had continued to be an avid reader and would suddenly discover an author and devour as much of his work as I could get my hands on. I was outgrowing what was available in the school library and was becoming an habitué of the local bookshop, 'Hempton's' in Shipquay Street. Having raced through Orwell and Steinbeck I was getting to grips with the more modern British authors such as Stan Barstow, Nell Dunn and their like. Modern Irish writers somehow eluded me, we had studied some Synge but I wouldn't discover Joyce or Beckett for some years yet.

I was encountering some of the more modern European writers too. Through studying French I was beginning to read works by Camus, Sartre, and some of the better-known French poets. I found myself drawn to Rimbaud, especially when I discovered that he had produced most of his best verse before the age of twenty. My thinking was knocked sideways when I read Sartre's first novel, Nausea. I found it difficult to understand and my understanding of it left me puzzled as to what on earth I was doing, or more accurately, what exactly I was doing on earth. It took me some time to get over it, but it probably served me right for reading it in the first place. After all, it wasn't on the curriculum.

My interest in sport continued to develop. I played rugby against other schools on Saturdays in autumn and winter and in summer I threw the javelin, discus, and put the shot with some modest success. Roy Seddon also formed a school basketball club which met at Templemore School, where we had the luxury of a real gymnasium. We played there on a Friday night before we set off, un-showered, up the town to pursue less sporting endeavours. Usually this led us to one of the church-organised youth clubs.

As the year wore on I found myself increasingly drawn to the social aspects of life and less and less interested in my studies. School provided little by way of guidance as to what might happen after A-level. We had a visit from the Army Recruiting Office and they showed us a film of what the army was up to in the Middle East, which didn't appear too savoury. Beyond that, I have no recollection of any information on what lay ahead of us post A-level. As far as I was concerned, there was the possibility of going to university or seeking employment locally. But what were the prospects? I couldn't see myself as a civil servant or an administrator in one of the few companies offering work. I most definitely wasn't cut out for a career in banking. My father came up with the notion that I might be interested in a career in The Metropolitan Police, an idea I rapidly dismissed. I resorted to my default setting: wait and see, on the off-chance that something would turn up

I should have been concerned about this lack of direction in my life but it was the Swinging Sixties, and whilst Derry might have been at best undulating slightly, the world was full of possibilities and so I was content to just get on with things. Essentially, this meant my attention was directed more to the social side of life rather than things academic. It was around this time that I found myself increasingly attracted to the world of music, especially the new obsession with Blues music which was sweeping the country. Some of my acquaintances from school had formed a band and I became a fringe member, that is to say I was allowed to carry equipment into venues, which had the great advantage of avoiding admission costs. I'm afraid we became a bit of a clique, immersing ourselves in all things to do with 'The Blues'. We listened avidly to the likes of John Mayall's Bluesbreakers, striving to outdo one another in our discovery of new artists, the more obscure the better, trying to be one step ahead of our friends.

Weekends were still taken up with school activities, mostly sporting, and in the evenings we went to dances. Most Friday nights there were dances organised in many church halls, and one we favoured was held in Bertie's Scout Hall on Distillery Lane, just off Spencer Road. It was invariably packed, necessitating an early arrival and probably a bit of queuing to ensure admission. On the downside, if you were fortunate enough to impress a girl so much that you were allowed to see her home, it could be a very long trek from her house back to Nicholson Terrace. It also required some judicious thinking on your part. I once unwittingly elected to leave a girl home who told me she lived somewhere near New Buildings. It proved to be a seriously long walk home on a winter's evening with sleet beginning to fall – 'near New Buildings' failed to convey that she lived nearer to Strabane than Derry.

I don't know how we coped financially. In a town like Derry there was no chance of a part-time job, given that there weren't enough jobs for people with families to raise. I think I got about ten shillings a week pocket money, sometimes supplemented by the odd half crown from relatives, leaving little spare cash to splash. Given that it cost around four shillings to go to a dance, maybe half a crown for a trip to the cinema, and around a shilling for a cup of coffee and a biscuit, we were always on the lookout for free entertainment. This usually meant sport, or just hanging out. We would walk the length and breadth of the town hoping for a chance encounter which might lead to some kind of diversion. Those long evenings usually ended in a cafe like the Dolphin on the Strand Road, trying not to irritate the staff and attempting to make a cup of coffee last an hour or more. Why this seemed preferable to sitting in the house applying one's time to study was a question which never crossed my mind.

Bizarrely, I had also briefly become a member of The Young Farmers Club, mostly because I was taken along by my cousins. The YFC had great social evenings which encompassed anything from Treasure Hunts to dances. That was fine by me and was more than adequate recompense for the evenings spent judging the milking qualities of cattle or the meat-producing potential of young pigs.

I had also become a football fan, which at the time meant a fan of Derry City, so many's a Saturday afternoon that was spent at The Brandywell. Derry could field a good team then and would be always there or thereabouts in the league. I never recall any sectarianism or trouble at the ground but there was always a kind of frisson when Belfast clubs would come to the Brandywell, especially visits from Linfield. I can also claim to have been there the night City beat F K Lynn. I was standing right in line when Jimbo Crossan scored that wonder goal from a direct free-kick, which sent the crowd utterly mad with delight.

With the benefit of hindsight, I am astonished at how little our acquaintances in those days stretched across the rigid sectarian boundaries of the time. We always seemed to hang out with people we knew from school and even that was bounded by geography – most of my pals lived within a few hundred yards of my house. I don't believe I had many friends who weren't in my year at school. There was possibly one exception which brought me into closer contact with 'the other side of the house', and that was my ongoing fascination with snooker. I continued to play in the GOH and through the game I encountered lots of people who were not Protestant, some of my own age, some older, and all of a diametrically opposed political point of view. Apparently, snooker transcended those boundaries. On one occasion a couple of thugs came into the hall trying 'to tap odds' from people. I didn't have any and they took a dim view of this before, on discovering I was one of the other 'sort', they decided I needed a good kicking. I was surprised that the rest of the people in the hall dragged them off me and sent them on their way. I was relieved and a bit pleased that I was considered to be one of the boys, despite my perceived religious affiliations.

I was more concerned about finding a summer job rather than working towards academic success. As luck would have it, one turned up: I was to start with Foyle Fisheries as soon as salmon season began. They had the rights to commercial salmon fishing on the Foyle system, which was a pretty big deal at the time. Salmon fishing on the Foyle was entirely dependent on the tide; nets were shot twice a day around low tide and this went on for the season. I think the salmon were given a free run up the river one day in seven, in an attempt to ensure stocks remained high. The fishing season began before school broke up for the summer. I don't recall how I managed to square that with school; I suspect I just didn't turn up and hoped for the best.

Fishing was hard work. We were based at Culmore Point and fished both low tides for six days a week. We rowed out to shoot the net and bring it round to a winch set on a sandbank, about two hundred yards further down the Lough. The net would then be winched in and any salmon caught would be despatched and packed in boxes, ready to be transported to the ice house on the riverbank at Victoria Road. I have few memories of the work – it was tough going and sleep was an issue, having to wake twice a day to catch the tide. The season lasted about six weeks and the wages were pretty good, so for once money wasn't an issue and I was able to splash out on trips to the cinema and random visits to coffee bars.

I think it was during that summer that I first began to think I might be quite reasonable at French. It appeared to be the only subject where I could make steady progress without stressing myself too much. As I alluded to previously, I had discovered the nineteenth-century poets Baudelaire, Verlaine, and Rimbaud. Somehow, something just clicked. I felt some kind of empathy, or perhaps it was because dropping their names into a sentence gave me an air of the arty, which then gave me the notion that I too might perhaps have a flair for writing. At one stage I really believed I might have some ability for songwriting and that this would somehow solve my dilemma over career choice, but it quite quickly became apparent that songwriting might necessitate some music. I had no expertise or ability on any instrument and anyway, most of the best songs might already have been written, so that dream swiftly faded. At the time I was overindulging myself in Leonard Cohen and The Incredible String Band, a kind of mixture of impending gloom with hints of depression and light whimsy. This lasted until the arrival of

Jimi Hendrix and Cream, who between them were enough to see me through the next decade or so.

Lower Sixth passed almost in a flash. In those days there were no public exams at the end of the year to focus one's mind on study, so I simply plodded along safe in the knowledge that so long as I didn't do anything outrageous, I could glide on to Upper Sixth which would postpone any need for decision making. The pursuit of girls played an increasingly important part in my life and since I had friends on both sides of the sectarian divide ,I thought my chances of success were doubled. With this in mind, Friday and Saturday nights tended to gravitate around public houses, not necessarily for drink per se, but more for the social side of things. In the beginning, young people gravitated towards The Castle Bar on Waterloo Street, but after some kind of falling out with the management people moved to The Mourne Bar in Foyle Street.

Essentially, 'The Mourne' was a dwelling house which had been converted into a pub, although I did later discover that it had at one stage of its existence been a hotel. (As it stood beside the very grand Melville Hotel, it must have been a very budget kind of operation.) Downstairs was the public bar, which was for the most part frequented by the older generation; it also had a television lounge where we might have watched football matches from time to time. Upstairs were a series of smallish rooms which each had their own regulars; these were almost defined by which school you attended or indeed which year you were at school. The Mourne was hugely popular amongst the youth and in my memory it was devoid of any sectarianism, although maybe it was favoured by students from Foyle above others.

So, Friday nights and Saturday nights were spent in The Mourne with most of my friends. Usually the weekend was punctuated by a game or two of rugby on Saturday. Why two? It was possible to play for a school team in the morning and turn out for a City of Derry team in the afternoon. If all went well, Saturday finished with a visit to the hop held by the rugby club in The Britannia Hall in Society Street. Being a good Christian country, the law stated that music must cease at 11:30 pm, so we all headed for home around midnight unless one had been lucky enough to 'get off' and thus have a girl to see home. In which case, who knew what time you might stumble into bed.

OOH LA LA!

I think it was in that summer that something else began to help crystallise my interest in French. Curzon Mowbray, our French teacher at school, was part of a group which ran student exchanges between France and the UK. One of the exchanges was centred on Derry, meaning that every summer a group of about forty young French students arrived in town for two weeks. For us this was utterly exciting and gave us an excuse to mingle with these exotic visitors under the pretext of improving our French.

In reality, it was a means to meet French girls. The students were placed with host families all across town, which afforded us the opportunity to visit areas we would never have had reason to go. We were delighted to meet these rather exotic beings and did our best to show them the highlights of our city. It also filled me with a desire to go to France and I at once embarked on a campaign to persuade my long-suffering parents to cough up the sixty pounds necessary for such a trip. Somehow or another I was successful, and for the next six months I had the anticipation of a trip to France to keep me motivated.

When the time came to set off, we were briefed by Mr Mowbray. Since it was not an official school outing, we were free of all school rules and regulations, so those of us compelled to smoke could indulge ourselves as much as we saw fit. Curzon had a plan of operation which would have done justice to the military. Everything was planned down to the last detail. It was a superb piece of management in which students from about a dozen different schools worked as a team to get us without mishap from Northern Ireland to the small town of Compiegne in northern France.

For me the journey began, as did most journeys in those days, at the Waterside Railway station. There were about six of us from Foyle, a few young ladies from The Londonderry High School, a couple of boys from St. Columb's College, and one or two girls from Thornhill. We used the two-hour trip to Belfast to get acquainted with one another. On arrival we made our way to the boat, which would transport us overnight to Liverpool. We were joined by about another twenty students, making us a group of about thirty. We took the train from Liverpool to London, where we caught a taxi to Victoria Station and entrained for Dover. Thence we crossed the Channel by ferry, having just enough time to eat our evening meal, and on arrival at Calais we took yet another train to Amiens, where we had about five minutes to detrain. The last leg we did by coach, finally reaching our destination at 10:00 pm, having spent about thirty hours on the move.

We were met in the town square by our host families, who were to be 'in loco parentis' for the next seventeen days. We were about three hours late, so we were whisked away in darkness to try and settle into our new abodes. Naturally the families had expected us in time for dinner, so when I arrived at my French home I was offered something to eat. It was the first course of the evening meal my hosts had prepared; I was offered a plate of 'salade de tomates'. I had never seen so many tomatoes so artistically presented in my life. I tried to do them justice before settling down for a good sleep.

Next morning I was awakened by the sound of traffic – it transpired that my house was located in the centre of the town on quite a busy thoroughfare. I made my way downstairs and sampled my first genuine French breakfast: coffee from a bowl and bread, butter, and jam. I'm still a sucker for it to this day. I did my best to overcome my natural shyness and made my first halting steps in real French. I was then driven up to the school which would be the location for the lessons we would have every day, from 9:00 am until noon. On that first morning we were all full of chat about our host families, how we had got on with breakfast, and so on. Mr Mowbray was most disturbed to hear that one of the families had been very cruel and had expected their guest to sleep in a cold room with no blankets. We were all a bit incensed and not a little apprehensive about this callous display, and Mr Mowbray set off to investigate. The host family were mortified – the bed had been made up in the traditional style, with the sheets tucked in at both top and bottom. My friend had not discovered that they had to be peeled back from under the pillows in order to get in between them. The hosts had simply assumed that he found the room too hot and had chosen to sleep on top of the bed. He was more than comfortable for the rest of his stay.

We had lessons in the morning, were free in the afternoon, and the evenings we spent with our hosts. I just loved the French way of life. I was particularly taken with their culinary habits – I loved the ceremony and celebration of food. It was Easter time and naturally Easter Day was an excuse for my host mother to pull out all the stops. The lunch began at noon with cocktails and nibbles, while the extended family had come along to welcome their guest from Northern Ireland. Ireland was a difficult enough concept for them – only rugby fanatics had any real idea of it – so the notion of Northern Ireland as a separate entity just didn't register. Easter lunch went on until about 5:00 pm, by which time I had to lie down. I was, as they say, replete. It was a wonderful experience which I have evidently never forgotten.

Trips had been organised for us both by our hosts and by Mr Mowbray. Naturally we visited the Palais de Compiegne and the railway carriage where the Armistice had been signed in 1918, but what we were all looking forward to was our two-night stay in The City of Light. We travelled to Paris by private coach, and as we arrived from the north there was great excitement as those famous landmarks appeared. We caught glimpses of Montmartre and the basilica of the Sacre-Coeur. It didn't take long to find our hotel but Mr Mowbray was not one to waste valuable time – we were quickly whisked off to catch a Bateau Mouche for a trip along the River Seine, which was an ideal way to get the bearings of all the famous sights of central Paris. Immediately after that we were off to The Louvre, where we got to see as much as we could in the short space of time allocated to us. Next we went to the Arc de Triomphe, where we were taken to the very summit. As we gazed over Paris, we could clearly see why it had once been named 'Place de L'Etoile'.

Following this visit we were given some free time to sample the atmosphere of Paris by strolling down the Champs Elysees, stopping to drink a cup of outrageously priced coffee in one of the many cafes which lined the Avenue. As we made our way to our meeting point on La Place de la Concorde I became increasingly aware that we were gathering a bit of a crowd. It was slightly nerve racking; surely Paris was accustomed to groups of students? Then it struck me that a couple girls in our party, one of whom whose hand I was holding, were wearing miniskirts. At home this would have drawn little comment but the fashion had yet to reach Paris. So, it transpired that our two young ladies in their rather short skirts were drawing lots of attention from passersby. Mr Mowbray, who had witnessed the event with some amusement, gave stern advice that such clothing would be ill advised at night.

After dinner in a restaurant we repaired to our hotel, whence some of our party went for an evening stroll, accompanied by Mr Mowbray. A friend and I rather foolishly had bought a bottle of ridiculously cheap wine, which we elected to consume in my room. This proved to be a very foolish move. When our group returned from their peregrination in central Paris, I was to be found going endlessly up and down in the lift. I could tell Mr Mowbray was not one bit happy, but his silence said more than any words could. Next morning, I paid the price of my excess. I filled myself with black coffee from the local café but all day I had the worst headache imaginable. I think that was the day dedicated to Versailles, which I enjoyed but not as much as I should have. Nowadays, when I think of Paris, I can still recall those few joyous days of Spring in

1967. It is equally astonishing to recall that the seventeen days we spent in France cost us all of sixty pounds.

As time trickled slowly along, it became increasingly apparent that all was not well in the town. Housing groups sprung up to protest at the terrible conditions many people were forced to live in. The Foyle College playing fields were adjacent to the perimeter of Springtown Camp, the former US military base. It had been abandoned by the military not long after the war and pressed into service to provide housing. Now, it was full of people who could find no other accommodation and who had been left to flounder by the authorities. On Wednesday afternoons as we played rugby, we would see children playing in the camp, but would have no interaction with them. We were separated by a strong wire fence, which was no doubt a relic from the war but seemed somehow to symbolise some kind of distinction between them and us.

Much later in life, I was to discover that a number of the residents of Springtown were members of the congregation of Christ Church. I was rather taken aback by this. I always assumed that members of the Church of Ireland were somehow more privileged than that, but on further reflection I recall that as members of the Scouts, we used to deliver parcels containing small items of food and a present to less well-off members of the parish at Christmas time. We left these into numerous households where there was little sign of financial wellbeing. I remember experiencing a slight sense of shock when dropping off those gifts at houses where there was no covering on the earthen floor and threadbare curtains on the windows. I suppose I had been protected from the notion that people in the mid-twentieth century should live in such a way. Our parishioners were nonetheless very welcoming and hospitable despite their straitened circumstance, and we were frequently offered cups of tea and homemade scones.

Sometime during my Lower Sixth Year, Granny had died. For a long time she had been pretty much an invalid, continuing to suffer from her rheumatism and from some gastric problem which prevented her from swallowing. Most of her days were spent in her armchair by the fire in the back room, from where she could survey most of the comings and goings of the household, as most visitors arrived via the back gate. It was from this vantage point some years earlier that she had asked my mother who the wee boy with the strange haircut who had just sauntered was. It was me. I had gone to get my hair cut and either on a whim, or because it was all the rage, I had decided I was getting a crew cut. The barber, Mr Hinds as I recall, was reluctant, but at my insistence carried out the task. I arrived home rather proud of my new look. Very quickly I was brought down to earth and put firmly in my place by Granny's scorn, not to mention the fact that I had rendered myself unrecognisable. Granny's death was my first close-up encounter with loss and I recall finding it difficult and upsetting.

Minnie, as she had been known, was quite a formidable lady, born when Victoria was still on the throne. Her father was an engine driver for The Lough Swilly Railway Company and they lived in a terraced house, the property of the company, which backed onto the railway line at The Collon. He was lured to the freshly emerging country of Rhodesia to work on the newly built railway. Unfortunately, he was never to return as he was killed in an accident, leaving his wife and young children to fend for themselves. The long and the short of it is that they were no longer financially secure and life became somewhat less comfortable. Granny went to work in service and remained there until the age of sixteen, when she fell in love and married Granda, who was considerably older. They began their married life in Granda's parents' house in The Lower Road. The rest of her life Minnie devoted to her family and the raising of her five children. The only fact I know of her early life is that in the neighbourhood she was the one summoned when some of the local ladies had difficulty in childbirth.

Minnie had had a rather large extended family, stretching from Manorcunningham in County Donegal to various parts of Scotland, mostly round Glasgow and Ayrshire. There was always a hint of lost grandeur in any of the conversations about the family, mostly built around her father's accidental death in Rhodesia. Apparently, one of our relatives had been stationmaster at Bridgend, which set us apart from other mere working folk. We knew little of Granda's people; at some distant time they had come into Derry from Carrigans but beyond that was a mystery. Granda never talked much of his background and appeared to care little about it beyond his immediate family, which included his brothers and nephews and nieces, whom he visited from time to time. He had several passions: he enjoyed playing darts which he did on a weekly basis in The Memorial Hall in Society Street, he also did some business with a turf accountant in North Edward Street. I think from time to time he would win a substantial sum, maybe fifty pounds or so, which he would contribute to the family finances. He also invested regularly in the football pools but with no great success.

After Granny's death life settled back into a kind of normality but, whilst we all missed her, Granda was inconsolable. He gave the impression of moving on with his usual air of unflappability, but beneath it you could see he was feeling her loss. I had never seen in their lifetime together any outward signs of affection but it was plain for all to see that he had been shaken by her demise. I suppose five children and fifty years of marriage stood for something.

DECISION TIME...

Before long, I found myself in Upper Sixth. It was time for making my mind up. School assumed that this was a task we could carry out by ourselves, without assistance from them. I vaguely knew what the options were: university or work. Only one member of the extended family had ever chosen university, all the others had found employment. What was available locally? Very little it seemed to me. I didn't feel ready to devote my life to banking or the Civil Service, which several of my friends had opted for. Given the subjects I was studying, the prospects in the government-funded manufacturing industries, such as Dupont, seemed out of the question.

The more I looked at it, the more likely it seemed that university would be the only option. Really this was only postponing any real decision-making for another few years, but sure, hadn't that worked before? Having made the decision I spent most of the autumn term trying to fill in the dreaded UCCA form. It was a nightmare. I had done little research into what I wanted to devote the next three years of my life to studying, so ended up with a random selection of courses and a personal statement which probably illustrated clearly what little commitment I had to anything. It was posted with a sense of relief that one more task was done and dusted.

Socially, life continued to be full of possibilities. For some reason Derry had found its way onto the map as far as visiting bands were concerned. I think that promoters saw Derry as a means of keeping acts working between weekend shows in bigger venues. We were treated to acts such as Lulu, Dusty Springfield, The Herd, and Peter Green's Fleetwood Mac, amongst others, usually in The Embassy Ballroom but always on a Wednesday night, which given Thursday was a school day was slightly awkward. I remember going to see The Who, minus Keith

Moon, perform in The Oasis Ballroom at Magilligan, as unlikely a venue as you could imagine. I think they played for about thirty minutes. Many of the locals who had turned up for a bit of dancing were more than a little nonplussed by The Who's repertoire.

About this time school had yielded to pressure and allowed some senior pupils to develop and publish a magazine, aimed at and written by the students themselves. I had pushed myself forward and succeeded in joining the 'Editorial Board', a rather grand title for those whose job it was to type up and print the actual copy. I think we managed to persuade some of the junior clerical staff to help with the typing, but running off the copy on the school's Gestetner was a nightmare. I wasn't content to be a member of the production staff, I wanted to be a writer, so I put myself forward as an entertainment reporter with the intention of giving myself licence to interview the 'stars'.

It was remarkably easy to turn up at a dance, declare yourself to be a reporter, and ask for an interview with the band. Cream, featuring Ginger Baker, Jack Bruce, and Eric Clapton were booked to appear in The Guildhall, so off I went. I hadn't the neck to try and gain free admission as a journalist, so stumped up the ten-shilling entrance fee. As soon as they had safely locked the money into the cash box, it was announced that Cream was unavoidably delayed and so would not be appearing. You can imagine the clamour that that elicited. We were offered our money back or we could stay and listen to a new group called Taste. A few of us decided to stay and we witnessed the first appearance of Rory Gallagher and his new band in the North. I was asked if I wanted an interview with Rory but as I had been expecting to talk to Eric Clapton, I declined. How was I to know just how big Rory was going to be?

Not long afterwards, I did get to see Cream. They were booked to play in Portstewart in the hall at the foot of the cliff, just below the school. Once again, I announced myself as a journalist and asked for an interview with the band. Cream were magnificent. When they finished, I was ushered round the back of the stage and there I was, standing in the middle of the band who, to be fair, didn't seem overly happy in each other's company. Ginger Baker didn't seem to know where he was, Jack Bruce was scowling and very unhappy, and Eric was pleasant but seemed keen to be somewhere else. I asked a few inane questions and was rapidly shown the door. I think that was the end of my career as an entertainment journalist.

As winter progressed, the applications I had made for random courses at equally random universities were answered, all but one in the negative. The only one in the affirmative was for a course in Ancient History at a college of which I had never really heard and had only been meant to fill a space on the UCCA form. I can't say I was really very surprised. Academic life wasn't really going that well and I wasn't sure I was cut out for it. I was proving to be rather good at talking but a little less able at doing. To make matters worse, our German teacher had come into money, decided that teaching and us could do without him, and set off to be a farmer somewhere in County Down. We were essentially left to teach ourselves for about half the year.

Upper Sixth was punctuated by two contrasting events. In late September, the school at Lawrence Hill caught fire. After more than fifty years the details are a bit sketchy, but I recall that it was quite a serious matter. It began after school had finished for the day, and the seat of the fire was thought to be in one of the Chemistry labs. Frank 'Sarge' Smith, the caretaker, lived with his family on the premises. Their accommodation was fairly adjacent to the chemistry labs and I presume it was he who discovered the fire and alerted the fire brigade. By a stroke of good fortune nobody was injured and I think we all turned up for school the next morning but were sent home forthwith. The damage was assessed as fairly light with no structural issues to worry about, so the school management decided the way forward was to use the pupils as the principal means to resolve it. We were instructed to turn up the next day armed with cloths and whatever cleaning products we could lay our hands on. So, bright and early next morning, a mob of young people set about washing walls and sweeping out dust and debris in order to get the school ready for action as swiftly as possible. Amazingly it worked: the school became functional and we were back to the grindstone within a couple of days. Mind you, the place stank of smoke and chemicals for weeks. Nowadays it would have been cordoned off for ages and we would all have been monitored for goodness knows what ailments.

The second noteworthy event was the transition from Lawrence Hill to Springtown and a brand-new school. We had been looking forward to this for years, mostly, from my point of view, because it would give us access to brand new sports facilities: a spanking new gymnasium and changing rooms with showers, what a treat! For months we had been brought out to watch the progress the builders were making and finally it was complete, ready to welcome the next generation of Foyle pupils.

Of course, it couldn't be ready to move in at the start of the school year, when all we would have had to do was walk in, sit down, and begin learning. Not only were we moving in mid-winter, we were also to be used to help in the move. I was lucky, I was assigned to help with transporting books from the old library in Lawrence Hill to the new accommodation at Springtown. Books were carefully packed into boxes, carried down two flights of stairs, stacked neatly in Mr Helliwell's Bedford van and driven out to Springtown, where they were carried up two flights of stairs and placed on the floor of their new home. I was astonished to see the treasures which had lain undisturbed in the old library. A first edition of Bedell's translation of the Bible into Irish is the one book which sticks in my mind. I remember thinking it was slightly incongruous that it should be there. But Bedell was a Church of Ireland clergyman and Foyle for most of its existence was a Church of Ireland school. That also explains why the Diocesan Library, now housed in its own purpose-built accommodation on the Magee Campus of Ulster University, spent at least half a century in Foyle College before the disestablishment of the church in the 1870s.

The move to Springtown was fairly seamless – we seemed to be in Lawrence Hill one day and Springtown the next – but the rules in the new building were endless. Shoes were the major issue. Our new classrooms had parquet floors which were highly polished, therefore school rules demanded that each pupil have two pairs of shoes, one for indoor use and the other for outdoor wear. There were rules about when you were allowed into school and when you were allowed in, there was a strict traffic flow. Some staircases were for up, others for down, but at certain times of day the rules changed and you were then permitted to use the 'up stairs' to go down. The greatest difference of all was that the school now had a canteen, which since Springtown in the mid-sixties was on the periphery of town, was just as well. Ladies came from the Department of Education to teach us how to eat. We learned the most efficient way to use a knife and fork, how to clear up after eating, and as a byproduct of this training how to eat as much as possible as quickly as possible, often to the detriment of younger members of the school. All of this was wasted on me as I continued to go home for lunch and a cigarette. I had it down to an art. Ten minutes home, ten minutes back. The walk helped keep me fit.

As the all-important A-levels loomed large, I began to get just a little worried. Had I studied enough? Did I really want to commit my life to studying a course I wasn't interested in at a university about which I knew nothing? I just didn't know. So I did what I always did: nothing. Well, that wasn't strictly true. I managed to find employment for the summer. A few friends and I had found work in a canning factory in King's Lynn in Norfolk. I had only a vague idea where King's Lynn was but who cared, another few months of my life were pencilled in and that was all that was important. No matter that my future, academic or otherwise, was by no means sorted. 'Something would turn up, didn't it always?' This appeared to be becoming the mantra through which my life was to play out.

Throughout my 'final' year I seemed to have a somewhat ambivalent relationship with school. In September I had secretly hoped to be asked to be a Prefect. I wasn't. I took it a bit 'thick'; I don't quite know why I was so put out. I was an active member of school, did all the sporty things, was a member of the Debating Society and helped out with the Dramatic Society, but alongside all that I wasn't particularly conformist and wouldn't have been behind the door on making my views known. To cut a long story short, I decided to form a rival organisation which I called The Anti-Prefect League. In reality, this so-called organisation had no structure whatsoever, was never formally established, and as far as I recall never did anything. It did seem to briefly fire the imagination of some of my fellow students, who thought it a vehicle for their rebellious nature. After all, it was the sixties and you had to be against something.

I have said I helped out with the Dramatic Society and so I did – it was a great excuse to miss a class. I might be called on at any moment to do some rearranging of the staging or run a message for so and so. The play that year was to be Hamlet and a great deal of effort was being put in by both cast and crew. I had been put in charge of the curtain. The play began in darkness as the actors made their entrance from the rear of the hall. On cue it was my job to open the curtain to reveal the scene on stage. Imagine my horror when the ropes became entangled, so as I pulled the curtain opened towards the middle, revealing myself and the stage crew hovering in the wings. To this day I can see the rage on the producer's face as he watched his carefully created atmosphere descend into chaos. To be fair, the performance was halted and when order was restored we started afresh, this time all went to plan. On subsequent nights everything went as it ought to and the production was judged to be one of the best performances the school had produced in a decade.

Life at school went on as normal but life outside school was heading in a different direction. Living in Derry in the early sixties had not been idyllic but it had been fairly stable and quite peaceful. Derry continued to be used as a NATO base; it was the hub for a school of anti-submarine warfare and as such the town would welcome ships from a variety of NATO members. It was not unusual to find the town crowded with sailors of many nationalities seeking a good time whilst on shore leave. Relations within the various nations of NATO were not always harmonious, at least as far as their sailors were concerned. Occasional outbreaks of fisticuffs might be witnessed on Derry's streets, particularly outside the bars frequented by the drunken sailors. These were rapidly broken up by naval shore patrols, often by the use of even greater violence.

Derry was also home to what we called 'The Yankee Base', a permanent deployment of American military personnel whose duty was to link Europe and the USA. Their living quarters were on Clooney Road and the actual radio station was on Dungiven Road, just behind the Irish Street housing estate. We continued to believe that the 'hotline' from The Kremlin to The White House went through Derry. We also felt some of the fallout from America's involvement in Vietnam as we watched it unfold every night on our television screens. At the beginning of the sixties we had survived the Cuban missile crisis and not long afterwards the assassination of President Kennedy.

Derry itself was becoming a bit less of the sleepy backwater that many considered it to be. The sense of neglect which hung over the city had only increased since The Lockwood Report recommended the location of the province's second university to Coleraine, and whilst some effort had been made to improve housing stock, enormous numbers of people continued to live in substandard accommodation. Given the disappointment of Stormont's decision to deny Derry the university, it was surprising that it was the housing crisis which brought people's disillusionment with government into sharpest focus. The residents of Springtown Camp had a sit-in protest in the Guildhall, marching into the Mayor's Parlour to draw attention to the housing conditions they were forced to endure. I should have known more about the residents' plight as Foyle College's playing fields had a boundary with the Camp and every Wednesday afternoon we could witness the residents going about their daily lives. Every week too would bring reports of various action groups leading protests against the Corporation. Whilst I was never directly affected by them, I was certainly aware that they were taking place and there was an almost imperceptible rise in tensions between the two communities. I don't recall this affecting me in any particular way; I might have been a little more wary in the centre of town at the weekend but in general life continued more or less as normal.

In June 1967, with my A-levels complete, myself and a few friends headed off to England to work in Donald Cook's canning factory in King's Lynn in Norfolk. I had no idea what I had let myself in for – it was to be my first time away from home fending for myself and I was a bit apprehensive. We set off for Belfast, took the overnight ferry to Liverpool, and caught the train to Peterborough and thence bus to King's Lynn. I was glad that someone in our group was familiar with the geography of England. After about twenty four hours' travelling, we finally arrived in King's Lynn. We had nowhere to stay but within about ten minutes we had found accommodation in what might loosely be described as a hostel, where we had bed, breakfast, and evening meal for two pounds a week. It was by no means luxurious but it was clean, warm, and for the most part occupied by young people like ourselves who had come from Ulster for summer employment. We were lucky: King's Lynn was used to a transient population and we encountered none of the discrimination which led boarding houses to display notices suggesting they would under no circumstances accommodate 'Blacks, pets or Irish'. I did nevertheless become 'Paddy' for the second time in my life.

When we turned up for work on the Monday at 8:00 am sharp we were duly signed on and issued with a timecard. We then discovered that the harvest had not yet begun and was unlikely to start for another week or so. It was our lot to be set menial tasks in order to keep us on site for when the harvest did begin and equally to get some work out of us to justify our wages. I was given a pot of paint and a brush and ordered to give the side of the building a good coat. Late in the day I was sitting on a rickety piece of scaffolding having a leisurely cigarette, when I suddenly found myself being addressed in upper-class tones by a gentleman about twenty feet below me. I wasn't quite clear as to what he wanted but the tenor of his voice hinted that he wasn't overly pleased with me. I made some kind of retort which was less than polite and my interlocutor stormed off, muttering loudly to himself. I later discovered that the owner of the voice was one of Lord Vestey's sons, Lord Vestey being the owner of Donald Cook's and much more besides. I learned he had been unhappy that I was having a cigarette at his expense and even more unhappy that he hadn't understood one word of my reply to his question.

A few days later when the harvest eventually began I was assigned to the reception area, where lorries arrived straight from the fields bearing loads of peas still in their pods, which we discharged into huge containers. I don't clearly recall what my role was but I made sure that at all times I looked really busy. The peas were checked for tenderness and then began their journey to the supermarket shelves. Firstly, they were stripped from their pods in a viner. After passing along a conveyor belt where any rubbish was picked out, they were then canned, cooked, and sent off to the packing area and thence the warehouse. When everything went smoothly, they were canned and cooked within a couple of hours of leaving the field.

We clocked in at 8:00 am; a lorry would drive around the town and pick us up if we were required to start early, otherwise we got the bus. We worked until 6:00 pm with an hour off for lunch and two tea breaks. We were lucky – the factory had its own canteen which allowed us the chance to get to know the locals and mingle with our compatriots, who hailed from all corners of Ulster. They were mostly university students interspersed with a sprinkling of sixteen or seventeen-year-olds like myself. There were some random individuals who turned up; I made the acquaintance of two young West African boys in their early twenties who were studying Psychology at university in Moscow. They were a great hit with the local girls as they claimed that they could read palms and tell fortunes. I was foolish enough to indulge them and permit them to read my palm. In a very matter-of-fact manner, they explained that my readings indicated I would be unlikely to reach the age of fifty. A bit blunt, I thought. I didn't take it seriously but I confess I did heave a sigh of relief when I woke up on the fourth of July 1999 aged fifty and a day.

Work must have tired us out as I have few memories of any exciting events taking place. In the evenings we watched television at our digs, maybe making the occasional foray to one of the local pubs and coming straight back to our lodgings. It never struck us that this was an opportunity to broaden our horizons or try and immerse ourselves in a bit of local culture. There were however three moments when I did try. The first involved poetry. We had learned that King's Lynn ran a literary festival and had read in the Sunday papers that The Queen Mother, who was in residence in nearby Sandringham, had been outraged by the appearance of someone or other who was billed to give a poetry reading at the festival. We decided this was an opportunity not to be missed and duly booked tickets for the show. On the night we were pleased to note the presence of a number of journalists outside the venue, ready to report on any salacious or untoward behaviour. We listened carefully to the various poets doing their thing but failed at any level to experience an appropriate sense of outrage. We withdrew to the pub to assuage our sense of disappointment.

My second foray into culture involved music. I had noticed that a little-known band called Pink Floyd were to play at a dance in nearby Downham Market so, seeing this as a bit of a diversion and possibly an opportunity to mix with some local young ladies, I boarded the bus which would take us to the dance. I knew little about the band but had heard their single 'Arnold Layne' on the radio and seen their LP in one of King's Lynn's record shops. When the band began to play, the audience was more than a little dumbstruck. They had come along to a dance but were presented with a group producing rather weird noises in front of a peculiar lightshow which was being projected behind them. I'm afraid the locals were none too pleased and it wasn't long before they began to express their displeasure. Soon, bottles began to rain down on the stage – there were no plastic bottles in those days. The band persevered for a minute or two but soon had to abandon the stage, leaving their instruments behind. I didn't expect to hear much more about them.

My third attempt at self-improvement was to go to the Cambridge Jazz and Folk Festival. I knew nothing about jazz but I knew a bit about folk so I guessed there would be some merit in it, and of course there would be girls. We knew Cambridge wasn't too far, forty or fifty miles maybe, so decided to try and hitch. We stood by the side of the road to Cambridge for an age. Eventually we were picked up by an elderly lady in a Land Rover who took us about ten miles down the road before turning off to a little village, where she left us. As she departed, she assured us we would have no difficulty making our way from there. Once more we stood by the roadside; this time we were astonished by the lack of cars passing by. We were in the middle of nowhere. After an hour or two of trying, we gave up. Eventually we got the local bus which brought us back to King's Lynn. I never got to the Jazz and Folk Festival.

Work in Donald Cook's continued apace and I was promoted to work on the seamers, the machines which sealed the lid on to the can. My job was to make sure there was a steady supply of lids and that the flow of steam to hermetically seal the lids remained constant. It paid an extra sixpence an hour, so financially it was worthwhile but it was a tough job as you had to be constantly vigilant. My final job was working at the cooker. This was a machine which rose about thirty feet into the roof of the factory. We worked on a gantry which was about ten feet from the factory roof. The cans were fed into a rolling framework which carried them round in a circle of sheet metal for about ten minutes until the contents were cooked. Our job was to make sure there were no blockages and that the steam was kept at a certain pressure and temperature. It was a two-person operation and by today's standards the conditions in which we worked would be illegal. At times you would have had to reach in between the rollers to extricate damaged tins, or use a hammer to unblock twisted tins from the machinery. It was the hottest spot in the factory but also the area where you were least likely to be bothered by management; as long as the tins rolled in and out you were pretty much left to your own devices. We were better remunerated because of the conditions in which we had to work, I think I was earning six shillings and nine pence per hour giving me a weekly wage of more than twelve pounds, an enormous sum in the mid-sixties. Towards the end of the season when many of the casual workers were moving on, I worked a shift of about thirty hours, beginning on Thursday morning and finishing on the Friday night at six. I couldn't believe my wage packet for that week – just over twenty pounds.

In the meantime, the examination results had been published. I only knew this because some of my better-off friends who had telephones at home had called their parents to find out. We didn't have a phone so I phoned our neighbours and got them to tell my parents that I would call back in an hour's time. When I called back, my mother read out my results – she didn't quite understand what they meant but unfortunately, I did. I wasn't going to have to worry any more about going to an unknown university to study a subject in which I had lost interest. One would have had to be very generous to describe my results as average. For probably the first time in my life, I was confronted with a problem with no immediate solution. What was the way forward?

My first instinct was to do nothing, so I put my dilemma to the back of my mind and got on with my work in the factory. It wasn't easy, as all my friends at work were busy making plans for the year ahead and I had to confess that I didn't have a clue as to what my future held. After some reflection, I decided that what I needed to do was to bite the bullet and find out if Foyle would allow me to repeat my A-levels. This wasn't entirely a done deal, as I would have to persuade them it would be worth their while allowing me to do so. Secondly, it would cost money, as you were only entitled to a maximum of seven years of secondary education. Having got that clear in my mind, I quit my job in Donald Cook's, as did most of my friends, and we prepared to spend our last night in King's Lynn. That in itself proved to be a bit of an adventure.

One of my pals had worn the same pair of jeans for the entire summer and they were rank, caked hard in a variety of juices from the factory. Indeed, they were able to stand by themselves in the corner of the room. He decided he would dispose of them rather than put them into his rucksack. Things got a bit out of hand and for some reason we set fire to his trousers; whatever had accumulated in the fabric, we suddenly had a conflagration in the bedroom. Being unable to extinguish said trousers we opened the window and tossed them into the street, directly into the path of a passing police car. In a flash, our room was filled with police officers itching for a row. Luckily, we were able to convince them it was a practical joke gone wrong rather than an act of teenage rebellion. We were fortunate not to end up with a criminal record. Suitably chastened, I set off with a couple of friends for a few days in London. It was 1967,

London was swinging, and we were so naive but terribly curious. We had made no plans and had no accommodation, we simply assumed that we would meet like minded people and be invited to join a squat or swept up in the Summer of Love.

I don't know what we expected: maybe lots of people with flowers in their hair or streets full of kaftan-wearing hippies. What we discovered was a big city going about its daily business, ordinary people doing very ordinary things. We hung around Piccadilly Circus and sat on the benches in Trafalgar Square, hoping we would meet up with people who would introduce us to this wonderful Swinging London. We set off to visit Carnaby Street, where I bought a kaftan. We looked high and low for the beautiful people who would transport us to another dimension, changing our lives forever. As the day wore on, we made the conscious decision that we would stay up all night in the hope of grabbing a bit of the action.

We wandered between Piccadilly and Trafalgar Square, took a turn up Oxford Street and along Regent's Street, down to The Mall. We thought we would sleep on benches in St. James' Park but were scared off by a crowd of youths who shouted at us. Eventually we went to an all-night café, where we stayed as long as we dared and then found a bench to call our own in Trafalgar Square. No sooner had I fallen asleep than I was awakened by somebody shaking my shoulder. He turned out to be quite a pleasant plain-clothes policeman, not much older than ourselves. He gave us some sound advice about sleeping rough and told us to be on our guard as there were gangs of pickpockets about, not to mention men looking for young boys for nefarious purposes. All told, I think I might have got an hour's sleep that night.

First thing in the morning we set off for Covent Garden, where we knew there would be cafés serving breakfast. It was there we met a young man who wanted to pay for our breakfast and offered to let us use his flat for a wash and brush up. Needless to say we declined both his offers, much to his chagrin. We had heard of this kind of ploy and whatever his motives, we were taking no chances.

I rapidly became conscious of how much of my hard earned-cash it was taking just to stay awake in London. I swiftly realised that the streets were not paved with gold and nothing was going to swing in my direction, so I caught the tube out to Heathrow and got a standby ticket for home.

THE CRIMSON BLAZER AGAIN

On my return to Derry my first task was to put my parents in the picture. They were going to have to put up with their son for at least another twelve months, that is if I could make my strategy work. I had had the foresight to time my return so I could head out on Friday night, so dressed in my newly acquired kaftan and beads I set off to The Mourne to meet my friends, regale them with tales of my exploits in England, and break the news of my intention to return to school. My one memory of that night was John, the proprietor of the pub, telling me that under no circumstances was I to reappear dressed in my kaftan or I would be barred. Obviously, the town was not ready for even the last vestiges of Flower Power.

On the Monday morning, I made my way down Lawrence Hill and hoped my plan would not crumble at the first obstacle. Mr Connolly, the Headmaster, was quite polite and listened carefully as I laid my ideas before him. He either was unaware of, or more likely was willing to overlook, whatever misdemeanours I had committed in the previous twelve months. I left with the understanding that if I managed to get the finance in place, I could return to school and retake my A-levels the following year.

My next task was to persuade the City Education Authority to invest in my education for another year. Their office was based on the first floor of Gywn's Institute in Brooke Park. With a degree of anxiety, I put on my best shirt and tie and set off to a meeting which could have a significant impact on my life. The interview took place in an office which might have remained unchanged since the days of Charles Dickens. I'm not sure I was all that persuasive but the outcome was positive and thus I had everything in place to get my career back on track.

So, having just turned eighteen, I scrambled back onto the great wheel of education. I didn't feel particularly out of place as I was now studying with students of my own age, having begun my career at Foyle a year younger than my contemporaries. To try and get myself off to a positive start, I had abandoned German and was now determined to sit A-level English in one year, having promised faithfully to read all the texts I ought to have studied in year one of the course. I was to persevere with History and of course continue with French. I was pleased to have been selected as a prefect, perhaps on the grounds that it might be better to have me for them rather than against them. Even so, I still harboured a slight resentment at not having been chosen the previous year. As far as I was concerned the main advantage to my selection was that prefects had a room to themselves, and also by some strange anomaly of design their own toilet, which was most advantageous if one had a sudden urge for a secret intake of nicotine.

One of my first actions on returning to school was to fall in love, my first genuine foray into the world of romance. Let me set the scene. Derry in the sixties was blessed with a fair sprinkling of Americans. First of all, there were those attached to the American Base at Clooney. Married officers were allowed to bring their families to stay and of course their children would attend local schools. Secondly, and slightly less numerous, were the families of construction workers and management employed at the Dupont plant at Maydown, whose children also attended local schools. They were for the most part based at the new housing development at Strathfoyle. It was the daughter of one of the Dupont workers who first won my heart. Strathfoyle at the time was really out in the sticks and whilst I knew how to drive, I had not yet sat the driving test. So, the only way to get to Strathfoyle was by public transport, which was somewhat infrequent, or by taxi, which consumed all my disposable income in one fell swoop.

As they say, love finds a way, and so most of my free time at weekends was spent at Strathfoyle, always with an eye on the clock as the last bus left at 10:00 pm sharp. During the week communication was maintained by telephone. Since we didn't have a phone at home, I spent ages at the kiosk in the heart of the Northland Estate, saying whatever it was that young lovers said to each other. It must have been quite serious because she was the first girl I ever brought home. My mother was pleased on the grounds that she was at least of the right religious denomination and my father got on with her father as they were both men with a military background.

School continued as usual. As I was repeating two subjects, things weren't too stressful to begin with and sure, English was only about reading a couple of old books, what could be the harm in that? I continued with all my sporting activities and managed a bit of courting at the weekends. I had begun to take writing a little more seriously and was beginning to get the hang of poetry and how it worked. I was heavily influenced by some of the American Beat Poets and I also took a shine to the Mersey Poets. As I said, there was quite a lively Debating Society organised by school on Friday nights, which gave me the opportunity to hone my use of language. I think I fell more into the use of histrionics rather than linguistics to get my points across, but debating did encourage me to think beyond the limitations of our narrow parochial boundaries.

School was proving to be a bit of a drag but I really was enjoying English. Mr Helliwell had a gift for making you feel as if you mattered and was very good at listening to whatever nonsense you were willing to put forward, gently pointing you in the right direction yet leaving you thinking that it had all been your idea. He also encouraged us to read widely around the subject and gave us pointers as to what was worth reading and what was not. He decided I was worth investing some time in and to that end he allowed me to order books I was interested in for the school library.

That meant I had the authority to go to the APCK Bookshop on Shipquay Street and place orders for books which I thought should be in the library. I can't imagine many students were given that privilege; I was always very careful to discuss my selection with Mr Helliwell before making the purchase. I doubt there were many school libraries with copies of Henry Miller's famous erotic novels, copies of Penguin Modern Poets, and the most up-to-date plays on their shelves. Incidentally, no one ever thought to steal them, indeed I'm not sure anyone other than myself read them. It was on one of those occasions when ordering some books that I found myself standing behind a rather distinguished looking man who was ordering six copies of Brian Friel's play Philadelphia Here I Come. It was all the rage at the time, playing on Broadway to great acclaim. The assistant wrote down the relevant details and then asked the customer for a name. 'Brian Friel', came the response. Without a flicker of recognition, the assistant wrote the name on her order sheet. I remember thinking that no matter how famous you are, Derry has always had a way of reminding you of your place in the world.

It wasn't long before the need to complete the UCCA form came around once more. This time I was much more focused on what I wanted to apply for and it was dispatched quite rapidly. I had decided that French was what I really wanted to study. I had applied to Queens in Belfast and considered it would do no harm to put in an application to the New University of Ulster, which was due to open in September 1968. With this chore completed, all I had to do was sit and wait for the offers to roll in. Before too long, one of the dull brown envelopes bearing the UCCA insignia came through our letterbox. I was of course an old hand at this business, so was pretty casual about opening it. As I perused the contents, I found myself rather dumbstruck. The New University of Ulster had in its wisdom seen fit to make me an unconditional offer to study French Language and Literature. This threw me into a bit of a spin – I had only been used to rejection and this had flummoxed me somewhat. It presented me with two difficulties.

The first, and the least urgent, was: did I really want to go to university? The second, more pressing, conundrum was: should I accept this rather unexpected gift? The second problem was a little more difficult. The UCCA system demanded that you reply to an unconditional offer within a certain time limit; failure to do so would lead to the offer being withdrawn. This offer was the first to arrive. If I accepted, I would have to withdraw my outstanding applications. If I withdrew, I would never know whether I would have received any other offers. I opted for safety, accepted my offer, and determined to make a fresh start in a new institution. Safe in the knowledge that my future was secure, I set out to make the most of my remaining time at Foyle.

Getting an unconditional offer may have settled my long-term problems but there were consequences I didn't foresee. Since my place at university was now secure, I was free to pursue my interests beyond the curriculum, which meant I spent less time on matters such as schoolwork and revision. I began to read even more widely, getting to know the work of the Beat Poets and trying to understand the plays of Ionesco. Inexplicably, I had become fascinated by Existentialism. Why on earth a wee boy from the Academy Road should become entangled in one of the great philosophical debates of the mid-twentieth century is anyone's guess! Even worse, as my interest in writing poetry grew, I conceived the notion that I might contemplate a career as a poet, ideally starving in a garret in Paris. The starving bit was readily achievable but the writing of poems people wanted to read was proving a little more difficult.

It was becoming increasingly obvious that things in the city were reaching an intensity I had not experienced before. There seemed to be regular protests over housing and employment issues and an underlying air of disquiet in the town, which led to deterioration in relationships between young people of different religions. Nonetheless, we continued to meet in The Mourne and go to dances at the weekend but as social unrest in the town increased, we began to be more careful when making our way home on foot at night. We would steer clear of areas perceived to be the domain of those of a different faith and avoid any confrontations with groups of strangers.

This of course proved to be a bit of a dilemma. If you were returning home from the Cityside it was straightforward, you simply went via Guildhall Square, up Clarendon Street and Bob was your uncle. Anywhere from the Culmore Road or Belmont direction presented no difficulties, you simply walked along the Strand Road and turned right at some point, but returning from the Waterside presented a problem. After crossing Craigavon Bridge, the most direct and therefore shortest route was through the centre of town via The Diamond, Fahan Street and across Rossville Street, up the Bogside, through The Little Diamond and home. Being lazy, I often choose the easiest and shortest route and, should strangers be sighted, I would cross the road and nonchalantly whistle what I hoped might pass for an Irish air. I was either very convincing or lucky, not once did I encounter the slightest hint of malice during my nighttime peregrinations.

Life took on a fairly settled pace. I was playing rugby at least once on a Saturday, playing basketball on the school team, usually on a Friday evening, participating in the Debating Society and conducting a fairly busy social life between dances and regular visits to The Mourne. As if that wasn't enough, school added yet another distraction. Several of the teachers decided that hill walking would be a bit of an adventure for those who were interested. So on Sunday afternoons, a minibus full of sixth formers, accompanied by several members of staff – usually a selection from Roy Seddon, Bob Leclerc, Stan Huey or Denis Helliwell – set off to walk in the hills of Donegal. Mostly we headed to Inishowen, frequently to the area beyond Buncrana where we would walk to the summit of Slieve Snaght. Not an overly taxing walk but on a good day it provided wonderful vistas over the surrounding landscape. Whilst the ascent was not too difficult the descent was even less so and we boys took advantage of this by running down the slopes and finding ourselves in the lounge of The North Pole Bar, with just enough time to refresh ourselves with a bottle of beer before the staff eventually joined us. By then, we were quietly sipping a mineral.

Meanwhile, my 'hands across the ocean' romance continued apace. Most Saturday evenings seemed to be spent in Strathfoyle and we appeared to be getting quite close. I was also approved of by her family, which was pretty unusual in my case. I was getting used to a kind of American way of life. In November I was invited to the family's Thanksgiving dinner where we were treated to the full works: turkey with all the trimmings and pumpkin pie to finish. All I needed was a baseball cap and I would be sorted. The mother of the house was also an avid bridge player and insisted that we should learn how to play. This was no hardship – I loved the complexities the game entailed and was eager to play at any opportunity.

I was getting rather set in my ways. Christmas came and went and life was great, I was getting on all right at school, romance was in the air, everything was, as they might have said in 1968, groovy. Suddenly the implication of 1968 dawned on me: not only was it an Olympic Year but it was a leap year. The implication of that was that during a leap year, ladies had the prerogative of proposing to their young men. Since this was the first time that I might have been considered eligible for the state of matrimony, I inexplicably began to take seriously the possibility of being proposed to. This just added another complication to my rather scattered existence. I decided I was much too young for this sort of 'carry on' and began to gently disentangle myself from romance. Not only was it causing me anxiety but I had just had the results of the mock exams and although I had fooled myself into thinking things were going well,

I had managed to conjure a pig's ear out of a silk purse. Knuckling down was what was needed and pretty sharpish too. I wondered if that was likely. I had made plans before but this time it would be different – I might just put them into practice.

Before I knew it Easter had come upon us. I had been invited back to stay with the French family who had hosted me the year before and I was only too delighted to accept. I travelled with Mr Mowbray's party but that really was my only official connection to them, which meant I was free to spend most days at liberty in Compiegne. I spent quite a bit of time immersing myself in French culture but I also sat for long periods in cafes, trying to look interesting, sipping coffee, dragging on a Gauloise and attempting to write poetry. I went with the group to Paris, this time avoiding the perils of alcohol. I also spent some time on my own wandering through the streets of central Paris and along the banks of The Seine. I got chatting to several young people engaged in precisely the same activity and was also propositioned by a prostitute. I made my apologies and beat a hasty retreat; I did learn some vocabulary which was unlikely to be much use in the examination room. In that Easter of '68 there wasn't an inkling of the disturbances which were to engulf France in a few short months. Once again I had enjoyed my couple of weeks and my notion of studying French, if I were to study anything, was reinforced.

The holidays were soon over and back at school I was facing yet another set of exams and my final season as a member of the athletics team. My forté lay in the throwing events, particularly the javelin and discus. We used to spend hours practising for inter-school competitions. We were all more or less self-taught, as no members of staff had any particular expertise in athletics. No matter how much I tried, it seemed impossible to make that all-important breakthrough. Then, on the final day of my throwing career, at a meeting at Portora Royal School, I had that moment when everything seemed to click. I took my run-up as usual and hurled the javelin with all my might. Lo and behold, it sailed out and landed legally over one hundred and thirty feet away. I was stunned – surely I must have broken the school record? When it was measured it came up some inches short; 'story of my life', I thought. It's strange how I have retained a much more vivid memory of that moment than of more important matters, such as the exams I was sitting at the time.

With the completion of the summer exams, I left Foyle for the third time. I had my unconditional offer, to which I had yet to fully commit. There was, after all, the option to decline it and re-apply to university through clearing when my results turned out to be as good as I anticipated. In the meantime, I had applied for a job back in Donald Cook's in King's Lynn. I was successful and this time I was travelling alone. I went straight to the boarding house where I had stayed previously, only to find that there were no vacancies. The next house I tried had a room and I settled into a comfortable three-bedded room on the ground floor.

I didn't have the room to myself for long. I was joined a few days later by two guys from Belfast called, as far as I recollect, Archie and Ciaran, students who also had just completed their A-levels. They were from St Malachy's College on the Antrim Road in Belfast. Before long we got to know one another and discovered that all three of us had an interest in literature, especially poetry. We all had jobs in the same factory but on different shifts. When our free time coincided, we would frequently sit and discuss poets whom we were aware of and try out poems on each other. They were much more knowledgeable than I was and made me feel a little uneasy about my ability with literature. They were easy to get on with and I wish I had kept in touch with them post King's Lynn.

That summer I was a little more familiar with the area and so frequented the pubs more often. Being a year older, I had gathered sufficient courage to socialise more with the locals. I became friendly with a local girl with the unlikely name of Perdita; she was slightly impressed that I knew the Shakespeare play from which her parents had probably chosen her name. I was impressed she even gave me the time of day. So impressed was I that I invited her out for dinner, another first for me. We met in the foyer of a local hotel and ordered dinner in the restaurant. Having twice visited France I at least knew my way around the menu and the wine list. The sommelier indulged my pretentiousness as I ordered a half bottle of red something or other. Over dinner I learned that she was at a public school and that she lived about five miles outside the town. After dinner, and about thirty shillings lighter, we agreed that I should see her home. I left her in front of a rather imposing redbrick farmhouse with matching outhouses, and quietly got back into the taxi which left me back into King's Lynn at no extra charge. I think the driver sensed my air of disappointment. I never encountered Perdita again.

I have few outstanding memories of that summer. France began to settle down after the student riots. Mr Dubcek headed the Spring Revolution in Czechoslovakia. As a result of the revolt in the East, two rather stunning girls arrived one day for work in Donald Cook's, creating quite a stir amongst the young men in the factory. I was still recovering from my foray with Perdita and admired the young ladies from afar. There also must have been a sense of revolt in the Norfolk air, as some of us became discontented with our work and transferred our allegiance to another canning factory about five minutes down the road from Donald Cook's. I think the factory was called Lin-Can but I can't be sure. My only certain memory of it is that it backed on to the river which flowed down to The Wash, the Great Ouse, I think. The embankment behind the factory was a great spot for a secret drag on a cigarette when things got a bit too hectic on the factory floor. We were less contented there as we were supervised much more closely, so we quickly discovered it had been a mistake to change employers.

As July turned to August it was again time to face reality and phone home for the A-level results. I had my unconditional offer securely in place but there was still a feeling of dread as I called home. I was glad of my offer as I listened to the results. My grades had improved slightly but once again I had failed to distinguish myself academically. Therefore, there remained only one decision to be made: 'The New University of Ulster', or employment. As usual I prevaricated – I still had a few weeks to make my mind up. I had the offer of a lift to Paris with a couple of local students who were driving to the South of France and there was also the possibility of meeting a couple of pals who were staying in a friend's flat in London for a few days. I decided I would stay in London and pick up the lift to Paris in Dover. I collected my final pay and set off to London.

The stay in London was no more exciting than the previous year; the only difference was that we had somewhere to sleep, but even that was a bit tenuous. It transpired that the flat wasn't actually rented by our friend but was 'borrowed' for an indefinite period. In other words, I was living in a squat. I stayed about a week, did all the things I had done the previous year, got fed up and went home. Once again London had failed to charm me.

Finally, as August drew to a close, I plucked up the courage and made a decision concerning my future. At the instigation of my mother I had arranged to see Canon Griffen, our rector. He was a part-time lecturer at Magee, where he taught Philosophy, and was the closest person with a knowledge of academia who would care to listen to my concerns. I have a strangely clear memory of our meeting. It took place in his car parked at the top of Clarendon Street and it lasted about five minutes. He was probably on church business and was fitting me in around more pressing tasks. His advice was clear and succinct. Basically, his premise was: 'If you don't go now, you'll never go. If you go now and don't like it, you can always withdraw.'

To me this seemed like sound advice. My mind was made up, it was university for the foreseeable future.

As September began, I decided to join my mother and father on a jaunt to Somerset. I think this was the first time they had ever had the opportunity to go on holiday together – it never crossed my mind that they might have appreciated some time alone. Somerset was the destination presumably because my father wanted to see his family once again and it wouldn't cost a fortune. We set off for Dublin in the family Ford Anglia, got the ferry to Holyhead, and motored down to Radstock. The highlight of my stay was seeing Canned Heat perform in Bath. They were high in the charts at the time with 'On the Road Again'.

After a week or so, I found myself back home bracing myself for the next phase of my education. The town seemed to be getting increasingly tense; politics seemed to be the main topic of conversation. There had been a civil rights march from Coalisland to Dungannon towards the end of August. It was initially very underreported in the media but seemed to gather momentum during September. I was too busy wrestling with my own problems to give it much attention; I was still trying to convince myself that university was the right option. Nothing had happened to change the course of my life, no one had sought me out to offer me a life-changing job. There was no letter from an editor wishing to sign me up for a publishing deal. The only letters from editors stated that whilst careful consideration had been given to my submission, it did not fit in with the publisher's current strategy. There was nothing else for it. I would sharpen my pencil and ready myself for further study.

Meanwhile, I went about my business as usual. I discovered that one of my fellow students from Foyle was also going to NUU, which lifted my confidence somewhat. A letter came from the university to tell me that my course would be taught at Magee, so no plans would be needed concerning somewhere to live. I have no idea whether I was pleased or displeased. Knowing me, probably neither.

Whilst waiting for term to begin I spent most of my time in idleness. I went to the pub in the evenings, by day I watched television. There was no idea that I was at a turning point in my life. In town, everything was plodding along. People were still bemoaning the lack of housing, the want of investment, and the general feeling of listlessness which pervaded the city. I was pretty well unaffected by any of that. My life was about to begin again, sure wasn't I about to become a student rather than a pupil? Things were looking up.

I decided I should take a look at Magee. It was funny that a place should have been there all your life but you knew so little about it. I hung around hoping to glean some information about what was going to happen and encountered some of the students who, like me, were about to begin their studies. I left none the wiser, there wasn't much of a sense of Fresher's Week. It must have been quite confusing for those students who were moving into second year at Magee. They were the end of the line – they would go on to graduate from Trinity. We were totally new in a new institution. We would graduate from NUU.

Lectures were to begin on Monday October 7th. I decided to spend the weekend with those of my friends who were not moving to pastures new. On Friday night I went to The Mourne, as usual. We had heard a lot of talk about a march being organised the next day, Saturday the 5th. It was to start from the Waterside railway station and proceed via Duke Street, Craigavon Bridge, eventually culminating with a rally at The Diamond in the centre of town. We hummed and hawed about going along to watch but eventually decided against it, thinking we might just catch the end when it reached the centre of town. I went home as usual just after closing time, bracing myself for three or four more years of study.

* * *